Nature Through The Seasons

Peregrine Falcon and Lapwing

Nature Through The Seasons

Peter A Gerrard

Illustrations by John Lord
Photographs by Eric Hosking, F.R.P.S.

MIDAS BOOKS

To my uncle John C. Gerrard, we shared an interest

m

First published in 1976 by
MIDAS BOOKS
12 Dene Way, Speldhurst,
Tunbridge Wells, Kent, TN3 0NX.

Cover design and illustration by Nikki Keep
Designed by David Morley-Clarke

Printed in Scotland by John G. Eccles, Inverness.

ISBN 0 85936 046 6

Contents

Page

SPRING – The Awakening Year 1

SUMMER 44

AUTUMN 91

WINTER 142

List of Illustrations

Adder and Grass Snake . . . 62
Badgers . . . 75
Berries of Mountain Ash . . . 147
Brent Geese . . . 126
Brimstone Butterflies . . . 43
Brown Rat . . . 120
Caterpillars: Puss Moth/Poplar Hawk Moth . . . 45
Common Lizard . . . 58,62
Cock Pheasant . . . 107
Coypu . . . 123
Cuckoo . . . 10
Dandelion . . . 94
Dormouse . . . 8
Fallow Deer Group . . . 103
Flowers . . . 49
Fly Agaric . . . 155
Fox . . . 160
Fox Cub . . . 109,111
Frog and Toad . . . 17
Great Crested Newt . . . 18
Grey Heron with young . . . 3
Grey Squirrel . . . 93
Hare . . . 82
Harvest Mouse in Nest . . . 141
Hedgehog . . . viii, 137, 139
Heron . . . 29
Horn of Plenty Fungus . . . 156
Insects . . . 90
Knots Flocking . . . 178
Larch Cone . . . 144
Lesser Celandine . . . 31
Lesser Horseshoe Bat . . . 38
Magpies . . . facing page 1
Mallards and Dry Reeds . . . 128
Mole . . . 41
Nuthatch . . . 4
Orb Spider . . . 158
Otter . . . 116
Peregrine Falcon and Lapwing . . . Frontispiece
Pike . . . 112
Polecat . . . 169
Potter Wasp . . . 86

Primrose 50
Ptarmigan 179
Ravens 130
Red Deer Stag 101
Rooks 133
Stoat 165
St George's Mushroom 33
Tawny Owl 174
Tracks in Snow 163
Winter Aconite 142
Young Rabbit 50

I wish to express my thanks and gratitude to all who have helped me over the years. In my search for a greater understanding of nature and the countryside I have gleaned information wherever it presented itself. My most valuable sources were farmers, gamekeepers and other practical workers on the land – men who were always willing to pass the time of day and allow me to share in their lightly worn knowledge of country matters. These then, and others too numerous to mention by name, while their contributions are unrecorded they are gratefully remembered. I am also indebted to my wife, for without complaint she allowed me to neglect my chores and escape to the woods and fields at all hours of the day and night.

Strong climber of the mountain's side,
Though thou the vale disdain,
Yet walk with me where hawthorns hide
The wonders of the lane.
High o'er the rushy springs of Don
The stormy gloom is roll'd;
The moorland hath not yet put on
His purple, green, and gold.
But here the titling spreads his wing,
Where dewy daisies gleam;
And here the sun-flower of the spring
Burns bright in morning's beam.
To mountain winds the famish'd fox
Complains that Sol is slow
O'er headlong steeps and gushing rocks
His royal robe to throw.
But here the lizard seeks the sun,
Here coils in light the snake;
And here the fire-tuft hath begun
Its beauteous nest to make.
O then, while hums the earliest bee
Where verdure fires the plain,
Walk thou with me, and stoop to see
The glories of the lane!

THE WONDERS OF THE LANE
Ebenezer Elliott (1781 – 1849)

Magpies

SPRING

THE AWAKENING YEAR

Although the first day of spring is officially listed in our calendars as the 21st March, this date bears very little relation to the actual time when winter relaxes its chilling grip and the growth of the new year gets under way.

As early as January, hazel and alder catkins, or *lambs' tails* as they are popularly known, are waving in the breeze and by February some species of birds are showing signs of courtship and mating, particularly thrushes and blackbirds.

The raven, probably because it is used to roughing it, living as it does on rugged northern coastlines and precipitous Scottish crags, is the first of our birds to begin incubating, for before the end of February it has paired, mated, built a nest and laid a clutch of eggs. Rooks do not lag very far behind, and may be watched in February pulling their old nests to pieces and collecting fresh twigs to rebuild or repair in readiness for egg-laying in March.

What occasionally befalls many of the smaller, early birds is that when a mild winter is followed by a comparatively warm January they are induced to mate and nest a little too soon. This is due to their mating instincts being geared to the weather; a sudden cold snap, possibly with snow, may result in the mother, along with eggs or brood, being frozen to death in the nest.

Bird song, although not completely absent in the months of winter, is certainly subdued. But by the end of February we begin to notice the more confident trilling of our residents. Robin, hedge sparrow, dipper, wren, thrush and occasionally the blackbird, may all be heard in this month. The well-known *little bit of bread – and no cheese* song of the yellow hammer is brightening up the fields and hedgerows and the pellucid cry of the skylark, reminiscent of cloudless summer skies, reminds us that spring is only the beginning.

Now, too, insects are becoming more evident. Some we may catch sight of on occasional warm days, others can be seen all the time for they normally appear in these weeks of early spring. The first butterfly of the year is either the brimstone, awakened from its hibernation, or the small white, the earliest of all our butterflies to emerge from its pupal case. The tortoiseshell, too, soon awakes, looking decidedly ragged around the edges. Caterpillars are rarely to be found in very early spring, but if you like to collect chrysalides, and keep them until the adults hatch, then digging in the thick moss at the base of trees usually turns up a few examples of larvae which fed on the leaves above.

A few flowers are out at all times of the year and even under the snow it is possible to find groundsel, chickweed and the occasional daisy or dandelion. Typical of early spring is the gorse, and although its finest array of colour does not burst forth until March or later, by the end of February its golden flowers line roadsides, motorways and commons.

Catkins, along with tiny lambs, are the familiar portent of spring, though some may have been visible even during the winter. Catkins are actually dormant flower spikes, and include not only those of the hazel, alder and birch which are particularly noticeable at this time, but also those of the various willows and the trees of the closely related poplar group. The *pussy willow* catkins found on the sallows are still in their first silvery stage and it will be some time before they open to display their glorious yellow. On the aspens we can see the long festoons of the male catkins – the females are much shorter and tend to hang down a trifle stiffly. That the two are different is no mere accident, the reason is that the males gaily swinging from side to side in the breeze brush against the females, which have less movement, and in so doing pollinate them. This, then, is the setting for springtime.

NESTS

Nests and the variety of their designs are almost as fascinating as the creatures that inhabit them, and spring being the period of great nest building activity, they are worth looking for, noting the type and comparing the different varieties.

Grey Heron *with young. Young herons leave the nest after two months. In the meantime they are fed by both parents.*

Nuthatch *at nest in an old wall. Note the use of mud to form the front of the nest*

Generally it is the female who constructs the nest, and in doing so she probably has to make from a thousand to fifteen hundred journeys carrying the grass, moss, twigs, feather down and pats of mud necessary to the building operation! Often she will be seen to fly a considerable distance only to return with material that would seem to be in plentiful supply around the base of her chosen nesting site. The male is not idle while his mate is so busy, he perches nearby and sings encouragement at the top of his voice and will even, from time to time, accompany the female on one of her journeys; but he makes no attempt to carry anything back with him. All males are not so lazy, and the sparrow and the woodpecker are good examples of species that divide the work equally between the two. To the other extreme goes the male phalarope, a snipe-like visitor to our shores from the Arctic. He not only constructs the nest of grass and weeds in a hollow of the ground, but when the four eggs are subsequently laid, he incubates them by himself until they hatch.

Anyone who has put up a nesting box in the garden to attract one or another of the beautiful tit family, must be aware that if the entrance hole is too big, sparrows or even starlings will take over the box, ejecting, if necessary, the tenants for whom the box was originally intended. So one cannot help but admire the ingenuity of the little nuthatch, who upon taking over a hole in a tree will, after cleaning out or enlarging the inside, plaster up the entrance with mud and gravel leaving an aperture only large enough for herself and her mate to pass through. This very successfully keeps out any other bird which might have piratical designs.

The most basic of nests is that of the nightjar for its eggs are laid in the merest of hollows on the bare earth, without even the luxury of a few blades of dried grass. All other ground nesters allow themselves at least a hint of bedding, even if their nests are generally not much more sophisticated. The reason for these almost non-existent nests is that were they more elaborate, attention of predators would be drawn to them. As it is, the eggs of these species, laid virtually on the bare ground, pass at a glance as pebbles. When the eggs hatch, the young fledglings are well covered with down and are generally able to flee the nest immediately and fend for themselves. It will be found that birds of this type are, like their eggs, camouflaged to such an extent that it takes a keen eye to spot them, motionless, roosting or incubating. Many times my heart has leapt into my mouth, as from immediately underfoot a pheasant, curlew or lapwing has sprung screeching into the air.

Birds that are more brilliantly hued tend to breed either in holes, as the kingfisher does, or else they cover their nests with a protective dome, like that of the magpie. Otherwise while they were incubating they would be conspicuous and therefore vulnerable. On the other hand, dull coloured birds build open, cup-shaped nests, while those which sport partially bright plumage generally wear it on the breast or lower edge of the wings so that when they sit on the nest their colours are hidden.

Not only the birds are constructing their nests at this time of the year. Mammals everywhere are equally busy selecting and preparing nesting sites for their young, although in many cases they are not nests in the true sense but beds or nurseries. Those mammals which go out of their way to construct a nest, specifically for the bearing of their young, are the dormouse, the red and grey squirrel, the rabbit and some mice. The remainder of the mammals, while still making provision for their litters, do so within the homes they have made for themselves and have lived in throughout the year. Animals such as the fox, badger and otter set aside a breeding chamber away from the living quarters, but nevertheless this still remains within their day to day accommodation.

The female rabbit, always jealously protective of her offspring, retires some distance from the main warren and digs a short hole which is usually from eighteen inches to three feet in depth. The end of this she lines with dry grass, and silky fur plucked from her own underparts. In this warm nest she bears from three to eight young rabbits, the number depending on the weather, the time of year and the availability of food. Should she become pregnant at a time when conditions are not favourable for the breeding of young she has the capacity, shared with few other mammals, of reabsorbing the unborn litter back into her tissue.

The doe does not stay with her young ones but leaves after each feed, carefully sealing the entrance each time with grass and earth, which is probably why these short breeding nests are known as *stops.*

These stops are usually very easy to find, for with each exit she makes, the doe inadvertently drags out tufts of fur, and where this fur is in evidence you are sure to find the nest. No flesh eater is fooled by the blocked up entrance, and invariably treats such nests as seasonal larders. Badgers are the worst offenders in this respect, for they will relentlessly work through an area by scent, digging out each stop and devouring the inmates.

While trees are still comparatively bare of leaves, the nests, or dreys, of squirrels may be seen quite clearly amongst the tracery of almost leafless branches. Those to be seen high at the top of the tree swaying precariously in the breeze, are the resting nests, loosely constructed and cup-shaped, although from the ground they appear to be round. In a smallish wood the squirrel may build as many as twelve to fifteen of these; none are completely permanent, for the squirrel uses whichever one happens to be the nearest when it feels like taking a nap. The breeding nest, however, is a completely different structure but again this would not be obvious when viewed from below. What is obvious, and should tell you which one to keep an eye on if you wish to observe the youngsters, is where it is placed. It is always firmly secured in the fork of the tree, or in an equally stout fork of a branch considerably lower than the sleeping quarters. With an intricacy that equals the weaving skills of any bird, pliant twigs, often with their leaves still on them, are tightly interwoven by the squirrel to form a ball shape, then the gaps are filled with moss and grasses making a completely wind and waterproof nest. Some dreys have been found to contain shredded rags and newspaper, so one can assume that any suitable material found in the locality would be used by the squirrel.

THE DORMOUSE

While hedgerows and bramble copses are less of a jungle than they will be later in the year it is a good time to look out for the beautiful nest of the dormouse. If you are lucky you may catch sight of the little mouse as well, for April is the time when they leave their underground hibernating quarters to begin living again. They are not as rare as is often imagined, at least in the warmer parts of southern England, but they are to be found increasingly less north of a line stretching from Cheshire to Suffolk. If it lives in Scotland at all it could only inhabit

The **Dormouse** *spends much of its active life among the branches.*

the wooded parts of the lowlands, and to my knowledge has never been recorded in Ireland.

Although that *dor* prefix to *mouse* is derived from the Latin word *dormio,* meaning to sleep, these little creatures are by no means dozy-mice. In fact they lead very active lives when fully awake, climbing high the branches of trees, scampering up and down in the twining stems of brambles and making prodigious leaps up to five feet or more, all in their busy search for food. Food is the main thought in the minds of dormice as soon as they awake, for after five or six months of voluntary fasting, they are considerably slimmer than the fat roly-poly animal that nodded off in October. Their hibernation is by no means a complete fast, for should there be a warm spell, and this is possible even in the heart of winter, they will wake up and tuck into the stores of food which were laid down for such an eventuality. No attempt is made to leave the underground nest however.

Secondary to fattening up once more, is the building or repairing of day nests. These nests, roughly about the size of a cricket ball, are made up of leaves, mosses, fibre and much broad-bladed grass, placed normally some feet off the ground and are difficult to get at such as in a prickly bramble or blackthorn. Being mainly active at night, they spend their days curled up in their nests deep in slumber, but as with most nocturnal creatures like the fox, badger or owl, it is not at all uncommon to see them out and about while the sun is shining. One which I came across while picking blackberries last year allowed me to pick it up and made no attempt to escape, in fact it was as docile as the tamest of pet white mice. In Victorian times dormice were popular pets.

The breeding nest is built late in spring in readiness for both a spring litter and, later, a summer litter. These nests may be recognised for what they are by their greater size, similar in construction to a day bed but a little over twice the diameter. Upon entering either kind of nest the dormouse closes the wall material behind it, like the closing of a door, making it impossible to see where it entered. If frightened, however, it will burst out at any point to swing away through the branches to safety, so should you find a nest that has an obvious hole in it you can be sure that it is empty for, as already mentioned, when occupied the nest door is firmly shut.

Often the dormouse is referred to as a miniature squirrel, and although they are in no way related, one can understand why early naturalists believed them to be a form of squirrel; an excusable mistake, for in their tiny way they are more squirrel than mouselike, not only in appearance but also in habit. Most mice spend some time in low trees while searching for sweet buds or berries, but the dormouse spends the greater part of its active life in the branches, so naturally has developed certain traits characteristic of its environment. Even its diet is the same as the squirrel's – beech mast, chestnuts, pine seeds, young seedlings. So if trees such as these are in evidence it strengthens the chances of catching sight of a dormouse. A less endearing habit of the dormouse, and one shared with the squirrel, is that of stealing birds' eggs and more than occasionally the taking of very young fledglings. It is particularly fond of the hazel nuts, a very high fat producer, which is just what it needs as winter approaches. To reach the kernel it does not crack the shell but gnaws a small hole in it, so small that it makes you wonder just how it managed to get anything through it.

Cuckoo *(adult male). Only the male of the species makes the familiar cuck-oo sound. Females have a ringing, bubbling cry.*

THE CUCKOO

A bird which never worries about where to place its nest, or in fact how to set about building one, is the cuckoo.

Although traditionally Cuckoo Day is the fourteenth or fifteenth of April, you should keep your eyes and ears open for these birds from the end of March, for there is no hard and fast rule as to when they do arrive, but they usually appear in all parts of the country at roughly the same time.

From the time of its arrival until it is ready to begin egg-laying the cuckoo spends its time leisurely acquainting itself with the layout of the area and, more important, selecting suitable foster parents for its future offspring. At first beetles and other insects are taken as food both in trees and from the ground but later, as caterpillars become more abundant, these are taken in preference, particularly the hairy caterpillars. Most other birds shun these, having found from experience that they are distasteful and mildly poisonous, for the hairs contain an irritant which can even cause a nasty rash on sensitive human skin, but the cuckoo never seems to suffer any ill effects.

Although they must mate to produce their eggs, cuckoos do not, as do some other birds, pair off for any longer than their mating time and seem to prefer a solitary unattached way of life. While they show no particular animosity to other breeds of birds, male cuckoos particularly will fight quite viciously with each other should their paths cross.

The call of the cuckoo is the most easily recognised and familiar cry of all our birds, yet what is not so generally known is that the traditional notes are only made by the male of the species. The female contents herself with a long, very musical, bubbling cry, reminiscent of the call of the laughing jackass. The male can also make this sound, so it is very likely that the cuckoo is heard on many more occasions than those of which the rambler is aware.

The reason for the cuckoo appearing to be in more places than one is due to its surprising turn of flight speed, a habit it shares with the jay, another erratic and highly strung bird, which seems to be constantly on the move. Should you wish to get more than a fleeting glimpse of the bird which makes that tantalizing call, the best plan is to sit tight once you have heard a cuckoo is somewhere in the vicinity. Sooner or later it will come within observation distance.

The cuckoo is not unlike the rock dove, but there is little likelihood of our confusing the two birds for each has a distinctive style of flight and pattern of movement. As already noted, the cuckoo is fast and erratic, whereas the rockdove, after an initial burst of speed, tends to slow down and fly in a straight line.

Though in flight the cuckoo appears to be a mottled grey, its upper parts are in fact a blue-ash colour, whilst its underparts are white, banded with dark grey. Occasionally, in some females, these bands are brown.

Having spent her time locating and making a mental catalogue of the various sites of nests where she will foster out her eggs, the female cuckoo is ready to lay as soon as these are completed and the unwitting foster parent has begun to lay. Without giving an exhaustive list of birds who are likely to be used in this manner it will suffice to say that the eggs of the cuckoo have been found in the nests of more than fifty different species in this country and these are always of the passerine type, or in other words perching birds, and within this group only the smaller varieties are used. Individual cuckoos tend to stick to the same species of fosterers year after year and, in turn, it is most likely that each successfully hatched and reared female fledgling will return the following year to lay her eggs in similar nests.

Having first removed one of the owner's eggs from the nest, by picking it up in her beak and discarding it some yards away, the hen cuckoo then lays her own in its place. In the case of domed nests, or those placed in holes, she ejects her egg into the cavity, but this is not always successful. The egg itself rarely excites suspicion for it is invariably a passable imitation of those already in the nest even to size, for in spite of the cuckoo's large build it lays a very small egg. Should the egg be discovered many of the intended fosterers would try to throw it out of the nest and, should they fail, then very often the whole clutch would be abandoned.

Laying of the eggs being timed to perfection, the young cuckoo breaks out of its shell very often a day earlier than the other eggs in the nest. But whether this is the case or not, the fledgling cuckoo wastes no time at all before tipping its foster brothers and sisters over the side of the nest. Nature, with an eye for detail, has designed the youngster specifically for carrying out such a deed, for in the middle of a broader than normal back it has a deep depression into which the egg or small chick fits very nicely while taking a pick-a-back ride to its death.

Within a very short time the fledgling fills the nest and foster *mum* and *dad* are kept continually on the go to quiet its shrill chirping by supplying food for its insatiable appetite. At three weeks it is able to fly, yet for another month at least it is quite content to remain in the nest and be fed by the fosterers who tend it without complaint. It has been noted that occasionally birds within the vicinity of the nest will also help to feed the noisy youngster and a case is known where a cuckoo was fed by a young thrush that had only just learnt to feed itself. Some people believe that the cuckoo has the talent of hypnotising other birds into feeding it – the truth is that the pitch of its plaintive demanding cry triggers off a response in the brain of other birds, which their maternal or paternal instincts will not let them ignore.

Gradually the call of the cuckoo is heard less and less, until towards the end of June the musical note alters for a time then ceases altogether, although the birds themselves are still with us. In July the old males take off to sunnier climes and they are followed a few days later by the adult females. The young birds often remain until mid-October.

THE FROGHOPPER

Whilst on the subject of cuckoos, it is worth taking a look at those frothy globules clinging to ferns and tall grasses which invariably make a mess on stockings and trouser legs and are known by the rather vulgar name of cuckoo spit. Responsibility for these blobs lies not with the bird but with an insect called the froghopper or, to be more accurate, with the larva or nymph of this species. The only association between these insects and the bird is that they both appear at the same time, but it seems that this was evidence enough for ancient country folk to make it the basis for a connection. Likewise two of our spring plants – ladies' smock and arum are also respectively known as cuckoo flower and cuckoo pint simply because their growth coincides with the arrival of the bird.

We have ten types of froghopper in Britain, and they range in size from a quarter to half an inch in length. If your eyesight is keen you are likely to find them hopping about in rough grassland during late spring and the early summer months, although their colouration of either green or brown makes them very difficult to spot unless, of course, you are having a picnic, then they make themselves obvious to a degree of annoyance.

In November the adults lay their eggs in the angle formed by a side shoot and the main stem of the plants and from these emerge the young froghoppers or nymphs. The term nymph is generally applied to the larvae of insects that have no pupal stage, which means that the young turn into adults without forming cocoons or becoming chrysalides. The larvae of moths and butterflies are known as caterpillars while those of true flies are called maggots or gentles.

Immediately upon hatching, the young froghoppers, by passing air through a sticky secretion in their abdomens, form around themselves a mass of bubbles which serve the purpose of protecting them from dehydration by sun and wind, and also as protection from their enemies. Young pheasants often choke to death after eating these nymphs, for even inside the bird's crop they continue to form their masses of sticky bubbles. Between June and November they turn from nymphs or naiads into adults and the need for the covering of *cuckoo spit* ends.

An exception to the above and the most often seen, at least in southern England, is the largest of the froghopper family, and presumably this is due to its pretty deep red and black markings which make it very conspicuous. This bright colouration, as with all insects that wear it, is a warning to birds not to touch, and it appears to be effective, for their numbers never seem to decrease. These froghoppers, unlike the others, do not make cuckoo spit, for while in the nymph stage they live underground and feed from the roots in the same way as their cousins do above ground, until they are ready to emerge as adults.

FROGS AND TOADS

While the froghopper is still lying dormant inside its egg, the warmer days of late February and early March have induced those creatures which bear the same name to forsake their winter hibernation and head post-haste to the nearest pond or lake for the annual breeding. This is the time of the year when you will see many frogs crossing roads on their romantic quest and unfortunately equal numbers squashed or maimed by motor cars.

Most people know what a frog looks like but what is not so commonly known is that although the basic skin colour is yellowish green, spotted and streaked with brown, this ground colour can vary quite considerably with individuals, depending upon the situation in which they are found. Different colours reflect varying intensities of light and the pigment cells of the frog skin contract under the influence of these reflections, so frogs found in a very dark loamy soil will, in effect, be quite different in colour from those found on soil which is rich in iron. This change of colour is in some respects similar to the chameleon, although the frog cannot execute this change as quickly as that creature, so one would not imagine this phenomenon to be used as a means of camouflage as it is with the chameleon. Toads are easily distinguishable from frogs by their warty, dry skin, which is quite unlike the smooth, moist skin of the frogs – toads cannot change their colour.

How frogs find their way to the breeding waters is not known for sure. Some naturalists think that they are guided by the smell of ripe algae which would suggest a suitable pond or lake, but others believe that many of them, who have hibernated not far from the intended site, reach it through their local knowledge of the surroundings. As it is generally the males who are first on the scene, their loud mating croak, in turn, guides or attracts the others. Unlike many other animals, there are no courtship rituals to be gone through – no preening, nor showing off – and the very loud croaking of the males, and the higher pitched chirping of the females, is not intended as a song of love for any one individual frog.

The fact that the male is a good bit smaller than the female, and has a coarse black pad on each forefoot, not only helps to differentiate between the sexes, but is nature's way of designing him for a particular mating function.

Approaching the nearest female, the male climbs on her back and clasps her tightly under the *armpits* or just above the thighs – the coarse pads giving him a grip that is almost impossible to break without seriously injuring one or other of the pair. Occasionally a number of males will try to take possession of one female and if the original suitor does not relinquish his grip, sometimes in the resultant struggle with the weight of three or four males, the female will be held under water until she drowns.

This pairing is the prelude to spawning, but the two may cling together for some considerable length of time before the female sheds the eggs. Even when she begins to lay, she does not drop them all at one time. As she sheds the eggs, often as many as three thousand, the male fertilizes them. This takes place in the water and the eggs then sink to the bottom, but as soon as the jellylike covering has absorbed water it swells and the whole mass floats to the surface as the familiar frog spawn which needs no description.

The mating and fertilizing technique of the toad is the same as the frog's but the resultant egg mass is different. The eggs are laid in a continuous gelatinous string often reaching the surprising length of eleven feet containing several thousand eggs, although this long string usually breaks up into smaller lengths. Once the eggs, like those of the frog's, float up from the bottom of the pool, the movement of the water soon entwines them around plant stems.

With both species, as soon as spawning is finished, parental responsibility towards eggs and resultant offspring is ended and they unclasp. The female leaves the breeding site to continue her life on dry land, while the male remains to fertilize the eggs of other females.

After four weeks the tadpoles hatch, but it takes another six or seven weeks for this almost larval stage to transform itself into a miniature frog – half an inch long. Most of us have at one time or another eagerly watched this fascinating life cycle taking place in jam jar *aquariums*, so it is unnecessary to describe in length the metamorphosis of tadpoles into frogs or toads.

Of the many thousands of eggs that are spawned, only a small percentage actually reach the frog stage, for they are a god-send to every kind of hungry aquatic life. Water birds, newts, fish and all kinds of voracious insects prey on them as soon as they are laid, and even if they survive their perilous infancy they are still in danger, for most meat-eating mammals are quite happy to add frog-meat to their diet. The toad has some protection against predators in that it secretes a poisonous irritant from glands under its skin, but this does not mean complete safety. The rat and heron, for instance, have learnt to remove the skin and thus avoid being poisoned.

The diet of the frog and toad make them beneficial creatures to have around the garden since you will not have to worry about buying slug repellents to protect your lettuces and other produce. Frogs and toads, apart from taking slugs, with a deft flick of their surprisingly long tongues, catch snails which they eat – shells and all – and earthworms which are much enjoyed, being held fast in the mouth by a lower row of tiny inward-facing teeth while they wipe down the worm's body fastidiously with their *fingers* to remove any soil or grit. The common frog may be found in all parts of Britain, but we do have two other species which were introduced to this country from abroad, although you are only likely to encounter these if your walks are taken in or around Kent, Middlesex or Surrey. The first introduction of the edible frog was made in 1837 around Norfolk, but it seems they have now sought a more southern climate. They are roughly the same size as the common frog, but you should be able to spot the difference between the two by the bright green colouring and a very distinctive yellow or golden stripe down the centre of the back of the edible frog.

The other immigrant is the marsh frog brought to Britain in 1935. It is over an inch larger than the common or edible frog and this fact, coupled with its dark brown colouration speckled with irregular black spots, should help in identifying it.

We have two kinds of toad – the common toad and the natterjack, both are widespread although the latter is not seen quite so often. Its loud shrill croak may be heard from some distance away, so if they are in your area you should have no trouble in being guided to their hiding place. Like the edible frog, the natterjack toad has a very prominent yellow line running down its head and back, but as the skin texture is so completely different, these toads being very warty, you should not be confused between the two.

Common Toad *(above)* **Common Frog** *(below)*

Great Crested Newt

NEWTS

Lizard-like in appearance and frog-like in habits, the newts – of which we have three species – are also on the move at this time, resplendent in their breeding colours. During the rest of the year they are drab and more difficult to spot.

Unlike frogs, newts have a prolonged and elaborate courtship, during which the male emits his spermatozoa in a jelly-like mass which sinks to the bottom of the pool. The female dives and takes this mass into her own body and by this achieves fertilization of the eggs inside her. She lays these eggs on the underside of aquatic plant leaves which are then doubled over to form a protective umbrella for the spawn. The development of the young newt is similar to the tadpole but takes much longer so that they are not ready to leave the water until the autumn. It has been known for late developers to remain as larvae in a pond throughout the winter, sometimes frozen into the ice and yet to emerge unharmed and able to complete their development later.

The larvae of the newt somewhat resemble tadpoles but they are more graceful, having a smaller head, a more elongated body and a longer tail. The external gills have a delicate feathery appearance.

There are marked differences between the three species of newts. The smooth newt, which is the most common but rarely found on mountain or moorland, is four inches long and has a prevailing colour of greenish brown marked with black spots. The underside is orange and also spotted. In the breeding season the male develops a crest from the upper part of his head, down his back to the root of the tail. The frilly edge of this crest smoothly undulates as opposed to the sharper serrated edge of the great crested newt.

The palmate newt, the smallest at three inches, prefers a mountain habitat and whilst being similar in appearance to the smooth newt, the difference can be seen by the unmarked flesh colour of the throat and a black webbing between the toes, which gives this newt its name – palmate being the zoological term for hand-shaped – web-footed.

The great crested, or warty, newt is more like the toad than the frog if one is making comparisons, for it too has the capability of exuding from its warty glands a noxious fluid as a deterrent to would-be predators. Seven inches in length, the name *great* is quite apt, yet, as large as it is, you are less likely to see this newt as often as you may see the others because it prefers deep water and some even stay in the water all the year round.

While amphibeans are more easily observed in springtime and perhaps are more interesting because of this, our ponds, lakes and streams are teeming with many other kinds of life, all equally intent in carrying out their individual breeding cycle.

GNATS

Even if the water you are peering into is not too clean or clear you are bound to notice multitudes of three-quarter-inch long creatures apparently hanging upside-down in the water. These odd looking things, with their long, tube-like, legless bodies, large round heads covered with tufts of stiff bristles and long forked tails, are the larvae of that pest, the dreaded gnat. A minute, but irritating, insect which can turn a pleasant walk into an agony of itching.

At this stage of its life the young gnat has to turn upside-down to breath because it draws in air through a siphon situated in its abdomen. By covering the surface of a pond with paraffin or a similar solution the growth of gnats and midges may be successfully prevented because the oil chokes their breathing tubes. Once it is in its next pupal stage this intake is accomplished by means of two tubes arising from the head which are thrust through and above the surface of the water. The head is now large and the body comparatively small and at a glance could be mistaken for that of a tiny tadpole. After some time spent in this stage the pupa is ready for its transformation into an adult, and although the change takes place inside the pupal form, the actual escape is carried out by the pupa placing its large head above the water line until it dries and cracks open. From the split in its outer covering a rather bedraggled adult gnat crawls, and after floating around on the raft provided by its previous skin, it dries, expands delicate wings and, if a female, sets off at once for a meal of blood. Males dine on the more princely fare of nectar. In most species of gnats it is only the female which draws blood and stings. So now you know that whilst cursing these miniature vampires you may do so in terms of feminine abuse.

To list all the forms of aquatic life which you are likely to see has taken up many a hefty volume and so just a few of the species that a springtime search might easily discover are mentioned here.

POND LIFE

Assuming that the pond water is comparatively fresh, you will see that it abounds with a legion of insects, yet not as many as you would imagine are solely aquatic. Many, like the gnat larvae, spend only their formative periods actually in water. Of those insects which are given over completely to a watery life, one that may be seen anywhere is the water boatman. What other creature quite so graphically lives up to its popular name? For to see this little bug skulling across the surface of a pond, using its two back legs in the manner of oars, does indeed conjure up visions of a vigorous boatman. The two hind legs, which give the impression of oars, are considerably longer than the two other pairs of legs which are situated nearer the head and are fringed with hairs, which act as a kind of web to increase the floating area as each stroke is made. These hair-fingers are obviously efficient, for a good deal of power is imparted with each rhythmic stroke enabling the *boatman* to shoot through the water in pursuit of tadpoles and even small fish, although it is only about three-eighths of an inch at its largest. No small creature escapes its interest, for with one bite of its piercing mouthparts it injects a poisonous secretion into the victim rendering it helpless. A word of warning – small fingers dangled in the water may be mistaken for a delectable meal, and the resultant bite, although not serious, will be quite painful.

If you watch the boatman closely as it skims over the water, you will see that it gives a little flip every now and again, then, hardly pausing in its progress, continues on its way upside-down. This habit has earned it another name of *back-swimmer*. The reason for this capsizing is obscure and open to conjecture, but if you observe the boatman for any length of time you may yourself find a possible reason for it. After all, much knowledge concerning wildlife has come originally from the notes of amateur naturalists.

One would not imagine that a skilful swimmer such as the boatman would have any use for wings, but in fact it is as equally proficient in the air as it is in the water and capable of flying strongly for quite some distance. Generally, its wings are only used to facilitate movement from pond to pond when conditions for it become overcrowded and cannibalism becomes common. Once settled in a stretch of water it does not seem keen on taking joyride flights, instead it folds its wings and forgets about them until such time as it is forced to move on. The wings are by no means a useless encumbrance in the water, for when it dives beneath the surface, creases between these wings serve to hold a small supply of air, and this, added to air bubbles which are trapped amongst the hairs on its body, enables it to breathe under water for some considerable time. These air bubbles lend a silver appearance to the boatman's normally brown and yellow colouring.

If you are particularly observant in early spring, you might find the cigar-shaped eggs of the boatman, for this is when the females lay up to a hundred, individually, in small slits cut in the stems of water plants. These hatch after about two months and the youngsters are simply a smaller version of the adult except that they do not gain their wings until later in the summer.

It would not be amiss to mention here the tough film which covers the surface of any water. To us there appears to be no such thing, but to the tiny creatures which inhabit any form of water, pond, lake or river, it is a very real factor that may to them be either beneficial or downright fatal. To a tiny insect this surface film is something like a sheet of self-sealing polythene sheeting stretched all over the water, and if we think of it in these terms we can understand why many types of larvae have sharp breathing tubes which enable them to puncture the film to get air. If they merely rose to the top, pushed through the film without puncturing it, then tried to breathe, they would die, tangled up in the dense skin.

The water or pond skater is an insect which makes full use of this skin or surface tension. Light as thistle-down, it is able to walk or skate over water without breaking the surface, although its second and third pairs of legs do actually *dent* the water, which if shallow will enable you to see shadows cast by these *footprints.* Although it looks very fragile, with its long thin body and six threadlike legs the skater is quite capable of seizing and killing large flies. Found in the same environs as the skaters are those creatures called water measures, which at first glance look very similar, but closer inspection will show they are much thinner in the body and slower in their movements. This slowness possibly gained them their name because of their apparently measured tread.

Named after an old-fashioned kind of spinning top, the whirligig beetle cannot be confused in its movements with any other water insect. Like tiny black beads, these beetles gyrate at an astonishing speed for minutes at a time, particularly when the sun is shining. If you put your hand out towards them they disappear instantly by diving under the surface, for although they can use the water's skin to support them whilst spinning, they are also able to pierce it at any moment to take refuge in the depths. As a form of defence, the whirligig can emit a very pungent odour when handled.

The largest and for me the most prepossessing of our numerous species is the great silver beetle. This insect may be readily recognised by its size, for it is in the region of two inches in length. Its colouration, which is an overall glossy metallic black, is also distinctive. When in the water, and covered with tiny air bubbles, it docs indeed look silver – hence the name – although out of the water the name *large black beetle* would be more appropriate. It is found in water-filled ditches and ponds well stocked with weeds and plants, for this beetle is completely vegetarian. The female lays her eggs in a papery, bag-like container, which she attaches to strands of weed.

In contrast to the placid and harmless silver beetle, the great diving beetle is a veritable tiger of the waterways, thinking nothing of attacking fish as much as six or seven inches long. Therefore it can be a pest, particularly in ornamental garden pools which it frequents, especially after dusk. If it is present in a pond, a quiet watch is sure to reveal it, for periodically it has to rise to the surface to breathe. It is a voracious brute when adult, and even in its larval stage it is equally capable of inflicting a very painful bite.

The larva is a creature with a curved tapering body, six long legs, and a bristly tail through which it breathes at the surface. As newts, fish and tadpoles are made painfully aware, it is equipped with huge jaws. The adult does not emerge as large as the larva – being only one and a half inches long. Apart from its ferocious habits it is a very handsome specimen with its dark brown or blackish body edged with gold. Male and female are almost identical, but while the female has grooved wing covers, those of the male are quite smooth.

The water scorpion, again a common creature, will also react violently if touched. Its name is derived from its elongated breathing tubes which curve like a scorpion's, but unlike its namesake, it is its other end you must beware, for it has modified its front legs into strong pincers for catching and holding prey – or fingers. Whilst walking about underwater on submerged plants it keeps its breathing tubes above the surface, but should it go too deep special sensory organs will tell it that its *snorkel* is about to be flooded.

One inch long, brown and with a flat oval body, it is quite unlike its cousin which is the long water scorpion, often known as the water stick insect, by virtue of it having the appearance of a scrap of twig or piece of straw floating on the water. These are not as common as the first mentioned species, although this could be due to the fact that their disguise is so perfect they cannot easily be seen. In some respects they are not unlike a very much larger version of a pond skater.

I hope that learning about our voracious aquatic life, does not spoil for you the pleasure of slipping off your shoes and socks to paddle in refreshing water after a few hours' hike.

While our waterways teem with various forms of insect life, both above and below the surface, there are many birds and mammals dependent on pond life for food.

THE MOORHEN

Wherever there is sufficient water to accommodate it, you will see the moorhen. Like the pigeon or sparrow, it is so commonplace that it hardly excites comment. Yet in spite of our familiarity with the moorhen, it is well worth taking a closer look, for its habits are fascinating.

You will be amused by the moorhen's comical way of walking, and this is how you are most likely to see it, because unlike many water birds it prefers walking to flying. When disturbed on water, it will almost run over the surface, churning up a great wake behind it in a noisy flurry that must make anglers tear out their hair. As one would expect, the moorhen is an expert swimmer and diver. It swims completely submerged by using the wings held half open to act as a rudder, as well as propelling itself with its feet. When it flies it does so awkwardly and has a habit of making strange nocturnal flights among houses and farm buildings for no apparent reason.

A nervous, clucking bird, marching this way and that, head and tail rhythmically jerking, like a tame or absentminded chicken, it will allow you to walk quite close before suddenly exploding into a frenzied panic.

Being so familiar, this black feathered *pedestrian* hardly needs description, but it has two outstanding features. These are the white under tail-coverts which are very noticeable when the bird swims with its short tail held up, and the bright red shield which is a tough horny skin extending above the red and orange bill. I have often wondered, but never proved the point, whether this curious plate is there to afford protection to what is perhaps a sensitive part of the bird's anatomy, for its positioning is not unlike that of the nose-piece on a Norman soldier's helmet.

This plate provides a distinct identification between the moorhen and the coot, the latter being a bird with which the moorhen is often confused, in much the same way as the stoat and weasel, or crow and rook, are confused. The coot has a much larger shield and this is distinctively white and apart from being heavier and faster on the wing these two birds are very similar in habit and appearance.

Essentially a bird of the water it is not uncommon to find the moorhen pecking around in the middle of an open field, or wandering through a wood, and in the same way its nest can also be found in unusual situations. I came across one in a dry roadside ditch, which was at least five hundred yards from the nearest water and another which was in the foreshortened branches of a pollarded willow. The normal situation for nests though, is actually on the water, and these may be built in the shelter of overhanging vegetation, deep in reeds or very often in the middle of a pool or lake, exposed for all to see. The nest is a rude affair of apparently roughly assembled twigs and is casually lined with reeds, rushes and other local plants. As new nests are often built on top of the old they can sometimes be as much as eighteen inches above water level.

The eggs, numbering from six to twelve, are buff coloured and speckled with red-brown spots, laid from March through until August. It is common for three broods to be reared in a season, which is probably necessary to keep the species alive for they are preyed upon by every carnivorous creature willing to get its feet wet, particularly the feral mink which is becoming a pest of alarming proportions. Those who breed pheasants and other game are aware that as soon as the moorhen can no longer be seen in their district, they had better get out their traps, for unfortunately this bird, so easily caught by the mink, is always the first to be annihilated.

While adult moorhens are not outstanding in appearance, the fledglings are attractive from their first emergence, as are the young of most of our water birds. Prior to the stage of assuming the familiar black colouring, which develops shortly after two weeks, the youngsters are brightly arrayed, having a blue crown, pinkish orange nape, orange bill and green legs. Completely confident in the water, they are able to swim almost from birth greatly assisted by feet that are larger than one would expect, and out of proportion with the rest of the body. The wings, at first devoid of feathers, have a hook-like claw protruding from the elbow and this assists them while climbing and scrambling amongst reeds and other bankside vegetation.

You are likely to come across these fluffy chicks from late March onwards and should you find a nest from which the young have just departed, keep your eye on it. A new clutch of eggs will soon appear and then you will be able to follow the whole laying, hatching and fledgling cycle.

Two of our more spectacular water birds, are the heron and the kingfisher, and they are well worth taking some pains to observe.

THE KINGFISHER

The kingfisher, with its brilliant plumage of metallic and cobalt blue, undoubtedly must be our most attractive bird. Many people imagine that it is comparatively rare, but this is not really the case, although the severe frosts of 1963 which froze almost every stretch of freshwater throughout the country drastically culled their numbers. This was a tragedy from which they have at last recovered. Due to its supposed rarity people think that the kingfisher is hardly worth looking out for and because of this many people miss sighting it. I have fallen into the same trap myself.

Upon moving into a cottage in Kent which had a very rural aspect, with a well-stocked river close by, I quartered and requartered the surroundings to acquaint myself with the local wild life. Believing that I could not be so fortunate as to have kingfishers in close proximity, I did not look for them, yet after some twelve months I came across a pair not eight hundred yards from my cottage. Strangely enough I had found their nesting hole months previously and had mistaken it for the home of a bank vole, which it resembled at the time. And in fact at some point it may well have been just this, for the kingfisher will take over any suitable holes in the bankside. Later, this same hole was taken over by a family of mink. In the spring the hole would not confuse anyone for it is typical of what one should expect from this bird. In marked contrast to the bird's beauty the approach to its home is disgusting. The nest itself, if it deserves such a title, is placed at the end of a long burrow and is no more than a litter of evil smelling fish bones and disgorged food pellets. On this rank bed, six to twelve delicate pink eggs are laid at any time between April and June. This nursery is a rose garden, however, when compared with the burrow tunnel and entrance, for down the centre of this runs a rivulet of slime and sewage composed of rotting fish. These conditions are usually at their worst, and naturally more apparent, when there are young ones in the nest. So your best bet when searching out the kingfisher is to follow your nose!

When one looks at a kingfisher's short wings and shorter tail and its disproportionate beak which gives it an unbalanced appearance, it is difficult to imagine that this creature can fly with an aeronautical poise equal to that of any insect. In flight its wings move very rapidly and it seems to *buzz* bee-like along so fast as to appear as a mere flash of iridescence. Spying a likely pool it draws up suddenly to settle on an overhanging branch or a projecting stump. Then, again in a cobalt flash, it drops to just above the water, stabs once and returns to its perch with a small trout, minnow or flapping bullhead gripped tightly around the middle by its dagger-shaped bill. Small fish are swallowed at once, but larger ones are first beaten on the perch until either stunned or killed, then, with a series of deft movements, the kingfisher turns the fish until it can swallow it head first. This is an intelligent safeguard against choking to death on the scales going down *the wrong way*. Having watched this operation it should help you to appreciate why the bird has such an apparently overlarge beak, set as it is in a small but very muscular head. The call of the kingfisher is a sharp medium pitched whistle when alarmed, otherwise it is a series of warbled whistles. Its bright colouration is worn for the same reason as that of insects and caterpillars, as a warning to predators that the flesh within the bright coat is foul tasting and therefore not worth the killing.

If you live in southern Scotland, the chance of seeing this brilliant jewel is rare. If your walking country is further north then unfortunately you are even less likely to see it. Elsewhere, however, and this includes Ireland, the kingfisher is there for you to find provided we do not have any more decimating winters for a long time.

THE HERON

With the heron, nature has been a little more liberal since it can be found in all parts of Britain. By this I refer to the grey heron, the bird which is generally associated with the name *heron* and not the bittern or spoonbill, which, although they are still genuine herons, are so rarely seen in this country that they hardly come under the scope of this book. Nevertheless they do appear in this country, but generally in the areas of game-keepered and fully protected reserves.

In appearance the grey heron is so unlike our other birds, whether on the wing or at rest, that you should have no difficulty in recognising it. If you think you have just seen a stork alighting in a tree or standing in the shallows, rest assured that you are mistaken and mark up *heron* in your nature diary.

This handsome bird, the largest we have that can be called *common*, is an avian fisherman of the lakes, estuaries and more overgrown reservoirs and is a particular favourite of mine. Like the rook, the heron nests in a colony, or, to give it its proper name, a heronry. These are situated in clusters of tall trees, near suitable feeding grounds, where the nests, immense structures of sticks, stand out against the skyline looking rather like very large rooks' nests. Although herons congregate together while nesting or roosting, they seem to prefer spending their days in a rather more solitary state, so you will not see flocks passing overhead. The pose in which you are most likely to see the heron is that of standing, sentinel-like, on the edge of a stream or in the muddy shallows of a pond, for, similar to the kingfisher, they wait quietly until some unwary creature swims by below them. A swift downward stab impales the victim on the end of a sword-like bill. Unlike the kingfisher which although equipped with a sharp beak only grips its prey, the heron does actually stab its prey, to catch, disable and kill. Large fish found mutilated on the bankside, and only half eaten, usually point to the presence of a heron and not to the otter. The latter tends to take a couple of mouthfuls from the neck and then discard the remains when not particularly hungry, and rarely mutilates the carcass in the same way as the bird.

Sometimes the heron can be seen striding up and down in the shallows and plunging its bill here and there into the water. This is likely to happen when a shoal of fish comes within its range, for then the need for patient watchfulness for a single fish is unnecessary. Apart from fish, it takes eels, water beetles, frogs, newts and, surprisingly, small birds. A naturalist recorded having seen a martin pierced while in mid-flight by a heron. The heron descended immediately and plunged the helpless bird into a water-filled trough two or three times, then swallowed it in a gulp.

When in flight, its large rounded wings flap so slowly and apparently leisurely, that until another type of bird can be seen with it for comparison, one imagines that it is very slow on the wing. This is not the case. Being light, but at the same time large, it covers a good surface area in the air, and so can soar and glide to considerable heights with very little effort. It also has a marvellous manoeuvrability, a great asset in enabling it to evade the clutches of its natural enemy, the falcon. Another enemy of the heron, although more of a pest than an actual hazard, is the rook and it is a common sight to see herons fleeing from a screeching, cawing mob of a dozen or so of these black highwaymen. Why this mobbing takes place is not understood, for they never seem to cause any actual bodily harm, apparently only being concerned in roughly escorting the heron out of their area. It is well-known that small passerines, such as blackbirds, thrushes and finches, will mete out this same treatment to any owl foolhardy enough to be abroad in the hours of daylight, and this with no retaliation from the victim, who flies peevishly backwards and forwards from roost to roost, until it gives up and retires to the gloom of its nest. All this one can understand, for these small birds are hunted down at dusk and even dragged from their roosting places by cruel talons, yet one could hardly place the comparatively harmless heron in the same category as the hunting owl. Perhaps there is an obscure reason that we shall eventually discover in the future.

Egg-laying of the heron takes place in late February or the beginning of March, so in early spring you might catch a glimpse of little groups of leggy youngsters preening themselves on the ground below the colony.

Grey Heron *in typical fishing pose*

THE DIPPER

Before we leave life in and around water, another bird essentially aquatic in its habits is the water ouzel or, to use its colloquial name, the dipper. It is known as this by virtue of the fact that it dips in and out of the water or, alternatively, from its habit of bobbing nervously up and down while *at rest.*

This bird is as common around northern streams and rocky burns as the sparrow is in southern gardens, where sadly the dipper's conspicuous flash of white breast is rarely, if ever, seen.

To a degree which few of our other water birds can equal, the dipper has adapted its way of life to suit the conditions under which it lives. So much so that you may observe it walk with deliberate paces straight into and then under the water, all the while pausing to turn over pebbles in search of small crustaceans and probing right and left as it snatches up passing tit-bits. It always walks upstream, for the shape of its slanting back is so designed that the force of the fast flowing water creates enough pressure to hold it firmly on the river bed. Unlike the kingfisher and heron, the dipper has no desire to prey on fish, and even if it wished to do so it is not adequately equipped, for although roughly the same size as a kingfisher, it bears no resemblance to it and is more like the pert and delicate wren in general appearance. Other than searching for its food in the guise of a feathered *frogman,* it also eats insects, caught by running and darting about on rocks and bankside. The nest is very difficult to find since it blends so well into the background, under a vast mass of green moss, dead leaves, heather bents and dried grasses looking like any other outcrop of vegetation. I usually find the nests by searching all the likely places in the vicinity where the dipper has frenziedly scolded me, with its sharp cry of *zit zit zit,* then flown away to return and perch on a rock, its white shirt front gleaming brightly, while it bobbed and curtsied with indignation. To search at random can be a long process, for these birds usually have a territory of anything up to two miles along the waterway.

Deep inside the outer camouflage, the nest proper is a shallow cup made up of grasses, and lined with leaves. In here, at the beginning of March, you would find possibly six pure white eggs, the first clutch of a normal three broods per season. Although their submarine activity is strange behaviour for birds, stranger still is the fact that the young of the dipper are able to dive and swim under the water with the greatest confidence even before they have learned how to fly.

SPRINGTIME PLANT LIFE

Although the snowdrop is generally thought of as a messenger of spring, it is usually well into flower while we are still huddled around the fire. For a plant that is so small and delicate in appearance, it must surely be one of our hardiest, suffering as it does January winds, frosts and snow. If you keep an eye on local snowdrops you will notice that they do not open until the day begins to warm up around ten o'clock, then as the warmth fades in mid-afternoon they close, but if the day is wet, or too cold, they do not open at all. It is amusing to imagine flowers as shops that open every day to allow bees to come in and browse around for nectar, although as bees are few and far between in these early months, the snowdrop often has to set its seeds with its own pollen before withering away.

The lesser celandine is another equally early riser, found everywhere – on banksides, outer perimeters of woodland and other places likely to catch plenty of sun. Small and golden yellow, it is very much like a buttercup, but having eight to twelve petals as opposed to the five petals of true buttercups, the difference is easily seen. Also it flowers much earlier than the buttercup. The name is derived from the Greek word, *chelidon* meaning *swallow,* but as it blooms long before the swallow graces our shores and has long since withered when it flies away, this connection does not apply to Great Britain.

Lesser Celandine

The lesser celandine must not be confused with the greater celandine, a summer flower of the hedgerows and waste ground, for although they both bear the same name and are both yellow flowers, they belong to different generic families. Incidentally, the stem of the *greater* contains a poisonous sap, deep yellow in colour, that at one time was believed to cure warts and relieve conjunctivitis of the eyes. It would not surprise me if it were true, but it is something I have not personally put to the test. Like many of our wild flowers, the greater celandine was cultivated extensively for its herbal properties.

The majority of early spring flowers, like the snowdrops, violets, woodruff, anemones, heliotrope and coltsfoot (which is a miniature dandelion) are usually to be found in woodland or areas where there is plenty of scrub, for here they can be protected from the worst of the weather. At the same time, while the leafless trees provide a very necessary protection, if these various plants did not grow, flower and set their seeds before the trees and bushes burst into leaf, they would suffer a very real danger of being cut off from the sun's rays and hence would never get much further than a few inches above ground. Have you ever walked through a beech wood in summer? If so you must have noticed how bare and lifeless the ground was, apart from ankle deep leaf mould. This shows just how effective the leaves are in preventing very much sunlight filtering through them.

Much less conspicuous, but nevertheless worth looking at, are two plants which are well into flower by the middle of February. These are the barren strawberry and whitlow grass. These names, however, are singularly inappropriate. The first is neither a strawberry as we know it, nor is it barren, as is proved by the way it spreads. However, this prefix *barren* could be a reference to the fact that whilst it physically resembles the strawberry, particularly at the flowering stage, it does not form or bear fruit.

Whitlow grass is not a grass, nor anything like it, but a fragile looking flower consisting of a rosette of rounded leaves from which a slender stalk, between one inch and five inches tall, bears a cluster of white star-like flowers. At a glance the blossoms appear to have eight petals, but a close examination shows that it really has four. Each individual petal is so deeply cleft as to make it almost two. A lover of dry places, it can often be found clinging tenaciously to old walls or with an equally stubborn foothold in shingle paths or shifting sand. As you may have guessed from its name, this plant supposedly had properties to sooth those painful spots which form under the fingernails. Many of today's wild flowers are named in association with medicine because in ancient times they were cultivated in gardens, not for their looks, but for the more practical reason of using the curative properties they contained. If a plant had no properties to make it worthwhile cultivating, either medicinal or culinary, then it was a weed to be ignored or at worst destroyed. Even the rose, pride of most gardens, was once grown principally for making a form of wine. Many plants, fruits and nuts were used to cure, or attempt to cure, ailments in those parts of the body which they were thought to have resembled; one example being that because the convolutions of the flesh of the walnut resembled those of a human brain, it was eaten or applied as a poultice as a cure for mental disorders.

Among the flowerless plants of early spring, the attractive silver green tufts and golden capsules of the thread moss are very conspicuous, covering as they do damp wall tops and old slate roofs. More striking still is the sulphur tuft fungus whose pale yellow flesh adds a small splash of colour to many old tree stumps. Most of the ten thousand or so species of fungi that grow in Britain produce fruit in Autumn so these will be mentioned in closer detail in the appropriate section. Of a few fungi that do fruit at this time the little *elf cup* is worth searching out, for it is pretty while young. As the name suggests, it is tiny and cup-shaped, but its feature is the red interior – a strong contrast to the white exterior.

St George's Mushroom

The four species of morel fungus are less attractive to look at but they do have an interesting shape, even if their burnt-ochre coloured cap is rather dull. An irregular, deeply honeycombed cap set on a short brittle stalk makes them easy to identify and is an advantage to people who like to eat fungi, for this type is edible, but if you are not too conversant – or to qualify this, one hundred per cent conversant – with the appearance of edible and poisonous types they should NEVER under any circumstances be eaten. During late summer and autumn we have roughly fifty species of the fungi boletus growing in our woodlands, so it is not unlikely that someone could find them and vaguely remember reading something about this type being edible and quite tasty. They may even risk cooking and eating them and get away with it because many are edible. That is, of course, until they happen across a species known as devil's boletus – a type not unlike the harmless cep boletus – then they are in very serious trouble, for when eaten this one causes, at the very least, violent convulsions and sickness, and at worst death. A sobering thought.

A most interesting plant, and one that is quite common all over the British Isles, is the cuckoo pint or wake robin – here again probably named because it grows while the cuckoo is with us. This plant is one which you will find interesting in appearance throughout all its stages of growth. In early March the leaves appear and are very easy to identify for they are dark green, shiny and shaped like an arrow head. The main feature, however, is that they are strongly marked with various sizes of black and purple spots. When these leaves are fully grown another leaf, pale coloured and rolled up tight like a long umbrella, grows out of the centre. Within the folds, and protected by them, are the actual flowers. After a short time the top two-thirds of this long leaf opens, revealing a stiff, purple spike-like growth. This is the flower stem, although strangely enough the flowers do not grow at the top as one would expect, but at the bottom, hidden from view and still protected by that part of the spathe, as it is known, which did not unfurl.

The flowers, if one can call them that, are peculiar in as much as they do not have petals but are simply small knobs arranged in tight rings around the stem. Above these seed-bearing flowers there is a ring of stamens, which are the male parts of the plant, containing pollen in their tiny heads. To crown this internal conglomeration, there are several rings of downward facing bristles and the purpose of these is to hold fast any small insect unwary enough to crawl within. The purple spike is not only a stem but also a lure, for by giving out a scent akin to that of decomposing animal matter, and having a bright colour, it has a magnetic attraction for small flies. Once alighted on the stem they naturally walk downwards, but inside, having passed through the bristles, they are trapped – and trapped they remain – until by their travels around this green translucent prison they completely dust the female flowers with the fertile pollen of the males. By the time they have carried out this involuntary task the spathe has withered and only then are they free to leave, no doubt looking like those cartoon characters of television fame, the Homepride flour graders, although covered with the yellow pollen instead of white flour. Undaunted by their experience they fly off to fall into the same trap elsewhere, hence spreading the fertile dust wherever they go.

Later, in July or August, the plant transforms into its last stage with the formation of berries, which grow in a thick cluster around the top of a stem, the whole looking like a short, knobbly, red cudgel. These berries are poisonous and can even prove fatal to children. Other names for this fascinating plant are arum, lords and ladies and, very apt, parson in the pulpit.

INSECT EATING PLANTS

While the cuckoo pint traps insects, uses them for its own ends, then releases them unharmed, it cannot be said to rank alongside those plants which not only trap but also devour. Most people are conversant with the venus fly trap a foreign insect eater sold in this country as a popular novelty. What is not so widely known is that growing in and around our own moors and marshy places we have three such plants which are equally carnivorous and quite as interesting, if not more so, than this imported exotic. These are sundew, butterwort and the remarkable bladderwort.

The sundew grows in the form of a rosette and is conspicuous due to its long stems, each with a single spoon-shaped leaf on the end, which are a pale orange colour. Each leaf has a border of fine long hairs and each hair has at its tip a globule of sticky matter, so they tend to sparkle when the sun shines. The surface of the leaf is sticky and this is where the power of the plant lies for when an insect alights on the hairs of the sundew, it is held firmly by the glue-like fluid, and as it struggles it sets up a reaction in the highly sensitive leaf. Slowly the other hairs bend towards the insect, holding it fast, then the leaf begins to curl until its two edges meet and the insect is well and truly imprisoned. In a short time the hairs begin to produce digestive juices for the purpose of breaking down and distributing the softer parts of the victim, but the hard parts – the wing cases and legs of beetles – do not break down and may be seen adhering to the leaves when it has uncurled ready for fresh prey. This plant may be found throughout the country, in bogs and marshlands, from late spring. In mid-summer it carries white flowers which stand tall, some way above the leaves. You might try keeping one at home for they flourish in a pot of peat moss so long as they are moistened every day.

The butterwort is found in similar locales to those of the sundew although it is less common in southern England. This is a very pretty plant, for the flowers, which radiate on long stems from a rosette of leaves, resemble the violet in colour as well as form. The leaves, which are fleshy and inward curving, are covered with a sticky secretion and although they are hairless, when an insect lands it is trapped in the same way as in the sundew. Should any other particles of vegetable debris, like bits of grass or moss, blow onto the leaves, they too are rolled up and dissolved.

Although declining in numbers, the bladderwort may still be found by those willing to search it out and is certainly worth looking for. A completely aquatic plant, it grows equally well in stagnant pools and ditches as it does in the wider stretches of marsh-water. When in flower the yellow blooms may be spotted standing erect on long thin stems well above water level, but normally, when not flowering, it acts as the true aquatic and floats midway between surface and bottom.

The term *leaves* can be a little confusing when applied to the bladderwort for they are not leaves in the true sense, but are hairy filaments appearing very much like the skeleton of a proper leaf after the soft vegetable matter has decayed, leaving only the veins. From the leaves hang many, small, brown coloured spherical shaped objects, and these are the bladders from which the plant derives its name and which are its means of trapping insects. Each of these bladders consists of a sac, on the underneath of which is a trapdoor fringed with bristle-like growths. This entrance is so arranged that when a small insect touches the bristles they open and the creature is sucked in by the slight inrush of water. Unlike the other two plants, the bladderwort does not overwhelm its victim with dissolving juices, but is content to wait until death from suffocation or starvation overtakes the insect, then, through very fine hairs which line the inside of the bladder, it gradually absorbs the decomposing remains. It will even trap tiny fish which are despatched in a similar manner. New growth does not take place on the stem, instead the buds drop off and sink to the bottom where they remain dormant in the mud until the following spring.

BATS

From plants that digest insects at a leisurely pace let us move on to bats – those mammals which catch insects at great speed while on the wing. As the warmth of early spring days induces insects to get up and about bats may be seen in gradually increasing numbers.

Being the only mammal that can fly, its physical manifestations are most interesting although rarely observed by the average person, unless of course it happens to be found roosting in an accessible loft, and even then it does not take kindly to being examined. Should you happen to come across bats in such situations do not be tempted to pick one up, unless you are wearing stout gloves, for they can give a sharp bite which, although no more painful than a nip from a mouse, can be a great deal more dangerous because bats carry various diseases which could be transmitted to your system through broken skin. The most virulent disease is rabies which is fortunately rare in this country due to our almost foolproof quarantine restrictions. When it does break out bats are often an important factor in its spread.

It was a long held belief that bats were mice which could fly, hence its country name of flittermouse, but they have no connection at all with rodents, being of a separate order known as chiroptera. The mistake is understandable, however, for discounting the wings, they are mouselike in appearance. The evolution of these wings is quite remarkable; they are actually the elongated fingers of a hand over which is

Lesser Horseshoe Bat

stretched a thin skin, this being an extension of the skin from back and belly. This skin is formed of two layers without flesh between and if you were to lay a bat's wing on this page you could still read the print through it. Adding to the mouse-like appearance, the whole of the body is covered with a soft silky hair which is particularly dense on the underparts.

March is the month when bats begin to be seen in any great numbers, for then they break their semi-hibernation. I say semi, because they do not go into complete torpid sleep during the winter, but the depth of their slumber tends to fluctuate in the same way as does our own sleep throughout the night. Should the temperature drop too low, they wake and fly around and in this way prevent themselves from freezing to death. So on a cold moonlight night in the middle of December you might catch sight of bats silhouetted against the sky.

We have fourteen species of bats throughout the country but in the main their habits are much the same. The most commonly seen is the pipistrelle – the smallest – for it is widespread even in heavily built-up areas. This little bat tends to fly high, dipping and wheeling in a very jerky manner and this flight pattern helps us to identify it. Natterer's bat is also widespread and again is easily identified by the fact that it generally haunts woodlands and flies fairly slowly about ten feet from the ground. The remaining species are not hard to find but tend to be localised – for example, the greater horseshoe, named from the peculiar shape of its nose, may only be seen in the hills of Wales and the West country.

The way in which bats find their way about in complete darkness was a puzzle to man for a very long time and probably helped to add to that aura of mystery that surrounds these creatures. As they move through the air on soundless wings, they emit ultra-sonic squeaks which are pitched so high that our ears cannot pick them up. Any object directly in its path reflects these squeaks back to the bat's highly complex ear mechanism and, from the speed at which the echo returns, the bat can tell how close the object is. Not only this, but it can also tell whether the object in its path is a telephone wire, a leaf or a tasty beetle. This method of *seeing* is often referred to as the bat's radar, but really the term should be sonar which is the use of sound waves for echo location as opposed to radar's use of electrical waves.

Apart from this silent (to us) squeak, the bat is at other times very vocal in expressing its emotions. This it does by squeaking at variable levels of pitch, many of these squeaks being low enough for us to hear and sounding not unlike those of the shrew though more drawn out. During discussions on bats, my mention of having heard them squeaking loudly as they swooped on clouds of gnats, has been met by others with mild surprise or tolerant disbelief, yet it may easily be proved if those interested enough like to go out and listen for them as dusk approaches.

When catching insects in flight, the tail and wing membranes make a useful basket for carrying and holding prey of a largish nature, such as moths and flying beetles which cannot be eaten in flight. Having caught an insect in its mouth, the bat spreads its legs out and forward so that the skin forms an aproned lap. By bending its head down into this *apron* it manages quite comfortably to restrain the victim until the bat can alight on a branch and render its catch helpless. Landing awkwardly curled, as it would be in this situation, is quite easy for the bat because halfway along each wing it has what remains of a thumb, now evolved into a sharply hooked claw used exclusively for clinging to surfaces. The nut-hard shell casings of many of the beetles it catches present no problems either, for the bat has a formidable array of teeth, which, in comparison of size, are more awesome than those of a tiger.

A sight worth seeing, particularly during a spell of dry weather, is that of bats drinking from pools, slow flowing streams, and even from roof gutterings containing some water. On the ground bats look most awkward, for after landing they propel themselves to the water's edge by using their wings in a peculiar shuffling motion. Moisture is more necessary to a bat than it is to any other mammal of similar size because as its wings are so large by comparison with the size of its body, it has a greater area from which its bodily water content must evaporate. This fact, linked with the fact that its staple diet of insects is comparatively dry, makes it necessary for it to get a plentiful supply of water.

Mating, which takes place in the autumn, is carried out while in flight. At this time hundreds of bats migrate together to find suitable mating grounds. Although the females are fertilized before they go into their semi-hibernation, lasting for four or five months, the female germ cell only partly develops then halts its growth. In early spring, following the winter hibernation, this partly formed cell, known as a blastocyst, becomes implanted in the womb and from then on growth is rapid – the young bat usually being born forty-four days later. Normally only one offspring is produced per year, although twins are by no means rare. In the act of birth the female hangs from a perch and catches the baby in the flight membranes of the tail, holding it in much the same way as she holds insects. The tiny bat, no bigger than a haricot bean, climbs up from the tail part, through the fur of the mother and secures a hold on one of her teats. So securely does it hold, it is able to be carried about quite safely, even while the female performs her characteristic aerobatics.

At fourteen days the youngsters are confident enough to take short flights on their own, although it is six to eight weeks before they are completely independent.

Naturally bats, like most of our mammals and many of our birds, plants and insects, can be observed throughout much of the year, but there are many facets of their behaviour or growth which are purely seasonal. Therefore it is a sound idea to begin watching the pattern of nature as early in the year as possible.

NATURE OBSERVATION

One reason for this early watching is that while there is plenty of material to hold your interest, it is not so great as to be overwhelming. Another reason is that if you usually take your walks or rambles in roughly the same area it gives you a chance to follow through various *finds*, such as watching kingfishers flying up and down the river bank under leafless trees, then discovering their nesting hole and,

Mole

later, culminating the experience with the fascinating sight of the young birds arrayed along a nearby branch.

I suggest that readers take a notebook and pencil with them when out on walks to jot down anything that catches the eye. For instance the first time you hear the cuckoo, or find your first nest with eggs, or even see changes in the state of the weather on given dates – make a note. Although it may not be apparent at the time, looking back over your notes can give you immeasurable pleasure, particularly when the wind is howling outside in the darker days of winter. Added enjoyment comes from those comparisons you will be able to make from year to year and at the same time you will have a record of when to expect to see the arrival of different types of birds; also when plants you noted are likely to be found and where, which is a great advantage. Such personal records will be applicable to your particular locality, for no single book can be sufficiently comprehensive to state all sighting times for the whole of Britain – it could only generalize.

Nature provides an inexhaustable variety of sights and sounds whether you live in the busiest town or the remotest village. Even the humble sparrow in town house eaves, the starling, the familiar pigeon and others are worthy of the naturalist's observation. Townsfolk do not think it is worth developing *country eyes* but if they did they would find plenty to see. Just off the main motorway to London Airport from Central London there are the sad remains of hedgehogs and frogs which have been run down and occasionally one may see the carcass of a fox – an animal which one is just as likely to see trotting along an inner-London suburban road as along a country lane. In fact you probably stand a better chance of seeing a fox in towns, where they are now quite commonplace, because they seem much less shy than their country cousins. In Kensington itself there are several families of jays and at least one pair of green woodpeckers. Badgers may be found quite close to the city of Edinburgh, while hawks nest on some of its higher buildings. Many varieties of mice, voles and shrews are no strangers to town houses or gardens and much of our insect life is equally at home there. So you can see that no matter where you live you will be able to study nature.

And so the first act of our annual four-act play is over. Yet there will be no interval while the scenery is changed, for like all good productions, once the preliminary build-up is achieved a cracking pace is set towards the main plot, or, as in nature's case, towards that season during which almost all the wildlife players are on the stage at once – summer.

Brimstone Butterflies

SUMMER

As spring drifts into summer it is not particularly apparent that one season has given away to another, for the changing pattern of wildlife habits and plant growth is as gradual as the darkness of night giving way to early morning light. Often the most marked change is that the warm bright days of late spring, which make us think we are already into summer, suddenly disappear, leaving in their wake sporadic showers of torrential rain. However, as consolation it is warm rain and quite unlike those downpours of October or February that make an outing even to the bottom of the garden a miserable chore. Apart from parching the ground and halting growth and germination, prolonged sunshine tends to dull the bright colours of flowers, desiccate leaves and coat everything with a fine film of dust. But what a transformation when those June showers begin to fall. Suddenly the countryside is bright green once more, everything seems to grow inches within a few hours and the *freshness* is almost overpowering. The heady fragrance of wild honeysuckle seems to reach out and grab you by the nose, for by now it has a good hold as it twines amongst roadside hedgerows of blackthorn and bramble, its pale orange-yellow flowers adding a delicate colour to the backdrop of greens.

Woodbine, which is another name for honeysuckle, though flowering throughout the summer, has two particular phases of growth and these are in June and September. Being a climbing plant it winds itself clockwise around the nearest stems within reach. This habit combined with a very powerful grip makes it a pest in woodlands, where the trees are being grown commercially, for by constricting the soft outer layers of young trees it cripples and distorts them out of shape, making the timber unfit for any use. A highly prized find, looked for avidly by old countrymen, is that of a blackthorn stem which has been distorted in this way, for the deep spiralled pattern makes it a rare walking stick. No doubt some countrymen, unwilling to trust to luck in finding such a stick, help nature along by giving the woodbine a little guidance up a suitable stem.

MOTHS

Woodbine is rich in nectar so is worth inspecting for the many insects that are attracted to it by its heady scent. Dusk is an ideal time for this inspection because as the night air dampens, that famous scent wafts across the lanes bringing night flying moths winging from all directions. The most spectacular are those of the hawk variety, recognisable by their large size and marked wing patterns. Mainly nocturnal, each of the seven large varieties of this moth which we have in Britain shows a preference for a particular plant when it comes to feeding, yet all like to supplement their diet with the nectar of the honeysuckle.

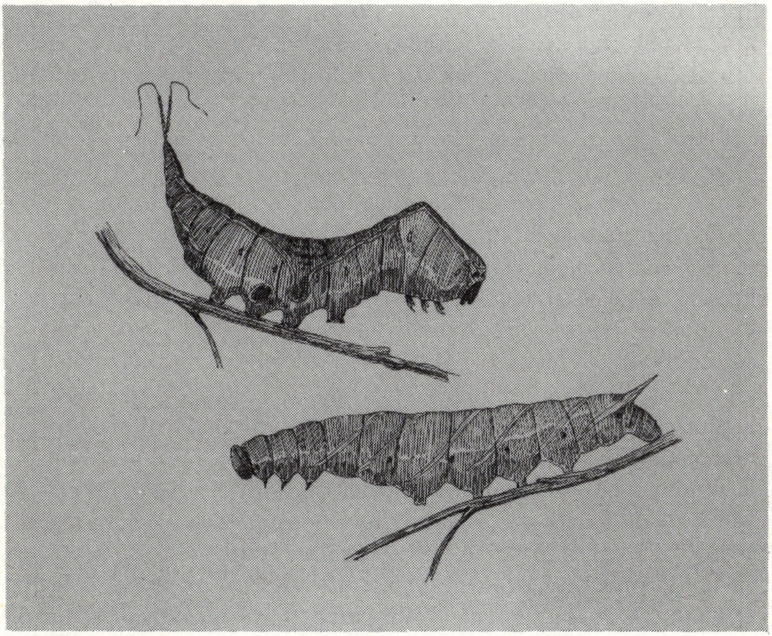

Caterpillars: Puss Moth *(above)* : **Poplar Hawk Moth** *(below)*

The lime hawk, and the poplar hawk, derive their names from the trees on which they feed, while the eyed hawk munches away at the leaves of apple trees. This moth is named from marking on its hind wings and when alarmed, perhaps by a predatory bird, it displays these figurations by pulling its forewings forward and the resultant two *large eyes*, supposedly not unlike those of an owl, soon frighten away the attacker. These three species are quite common, but when they are at rest with wings folded they look remarkably like dead leaves, so it takes a keen eye to search them out.

Knowing the feeding habits of moths and butterflies and other types of insects is almost a guarantee of finding the species you are most interested in, assuming that their particular food-plant is growing in your area. When their names are linked with certain plants, remembering these names is made so much easier, although if you were to search through a hedgerow of privet for the largest of our hawk moths, the privet hawk, you would be searching in vain for they feed solely on lilac. The elephant hawk moth gets its name from its caterpillar which has a habit of extending its head and neck when alarmed so that it appears like an elephant trunk. This moth also borrows a deterrent from the eyed hawk for it, too, has eye-like marking on its thorax which it can swell up to frighten birds away. These may be found on the bedstraws, low growing plants easily recognised because of their thin, square stems that trail over the ground, bearing whorls of four to twelve leaves and clusters of tiny flowers. Of the dozen or so native species, there seems to be at least one for most types of habitat: to name but three – hedge bedstraw, marsh bedstraw and heath bedstraw.

Another hawk, whose caterpillar may be found exclusively on bedstraws, is the humming bird hawk, but as it is a migrant the caterpillar would only be found on the rare occasions that the moth had bred in this country. This moth is very aptly named and many people have made the mistake of thinking they have seen a real humming bird in Britain. One and a half inches in length, with an equally long tongue which it unfolds to drink nectar from flowers while on the wing, at a glance it looks just like a hovering humming bird.

The death's head hawk moth is much prized by all serious collectors of moths for though not rare, it is certainly the most famous, and one that can be confused with no other because the markings on the thorax resemble a perfect human skull. The eyes of this *skull* show blue black on a ground of yellow brown.

Many people are confused between moths and butterflies, yet the simplest way of telling the difference is that moths have antennae or feelers that are feathery, while those of the butterfly are slender, and have a small knob on the end. Although *feelers* are a generally accepted term for the antennae of both species, they are in fact not organs of touch, but of smell. Another difference is that moths fan their wings out when at rest, while butterflies rest with the upper surfaces of their wings meeting over the back.

Some reference books state that moths are *dull coloured night fliers,* yet there are many moths that are exceptions to the nocturnal habit and even more that sport bright colours. As I write I have close by me three very beautiful moths which, as if wishing a mention in the text, have flown through the window within the last ten minutes. The largest, which is some two inches across, is unmistakably a swallowtail, for it has projections from its hind wings which are characteristic of this species and is a very pale greenish yellow. The second is also a swallowtail but is only half the size. At a glance it appears pale grey, but a closer inspection reveals that it has a tinge of yellow, brown and green on the wings which are also edged with red. Swallowtails may be found from July through until autumn. Earlier than this their strange twig-like caterpillars may be found on hawthorn or privet. Both these moths are resting with their wings spread out, but my third visitor has its wings folded along its body giving it the appearance of a leaf. This one is the lime hawk which I have already mentioned, and in the flesh the almost fluorescent lime-green markings on its wings seem to glow in a way that no text book illustration could possibly capture.

Looking around my study these three are the most notable but there must be at least another twenty-five of the smaller and less colourful varieties which have also flown in the window.

Should you be disappointed by the number of night fliers that visit your garden or window, try encouraging them with a tit-bit they cannot resist. Books specializing on the subject of moths and butterflies give various recipes for this *sugaring*, as it is known, which consists of molasses, strong beer and other refinements. But if you simply wish to try out the idea, I can assure your success if you paint treacle or syrup onto a piece of wood then prop this against your lighted window. If the evening is warm and dry, in no time at all you will find many moths and other insects clustered around the outside of the liquid, dipping their long tongues into what to them is nectar, all the time sure that their legs and wings are well out of the sticky food.

SUMMER FLOWERS

What a difference a few days of intermittent rain and very hot June sunshine can make to trees and flowers. Suddenly the countryside sparkles with the effect of brilliant colours against many shades of green. A plant which is much in evidence is the ramson, though this is not due to its spectacular appearance, but rather the fact that wherever you walk, along the riverbank or in the shadier parts of the woods, your nostrils are assailed by the very strong scent of garlic, hence its more common name of wild garlic. Though I am only guessing, I would imagine that long ago this plant was used as well as, or in place of, onions – and I have heard that bread made from wheat cut from the damp edges of fields very often had a not unpleasant taste of onions, because the reaper had scythed up a fair portion of ramsons and never troubled to clean them out.

With their long shiny leaves and clusters of white star-like flowers ramsons make a pleasant backdrop for bluebells which generally grow in the same areas, both carpeting the damp woodland ground. In two separate woods where I often walk, great areas of these plants are laid flat as though steamrollered and the reason for this I will explain later.

What a variety of flowers abound – dog rose, buttercup and poppy, the tiny birdsfoot trefoil which adds a glorious sprinkling of yellow to meadowland, tall and stately foxgloves flowering from the bottom of the stem upwards until the final bloom stands high above its withered predecessors; purple sheepsbit, red montbretia, yellow catsear, white bindweed (curse of every gardener), blue toadflax, the pale green of pineapple mayweed and fat hen – an amusing name for a plant whose seeds, high in fat content, were a source of food from prehistoric times until the 19th century. Along the river bank, again more colour, as white arrowhead, pink bistort, purple cinquefoil and deep yellow water lily, vie for your attention.

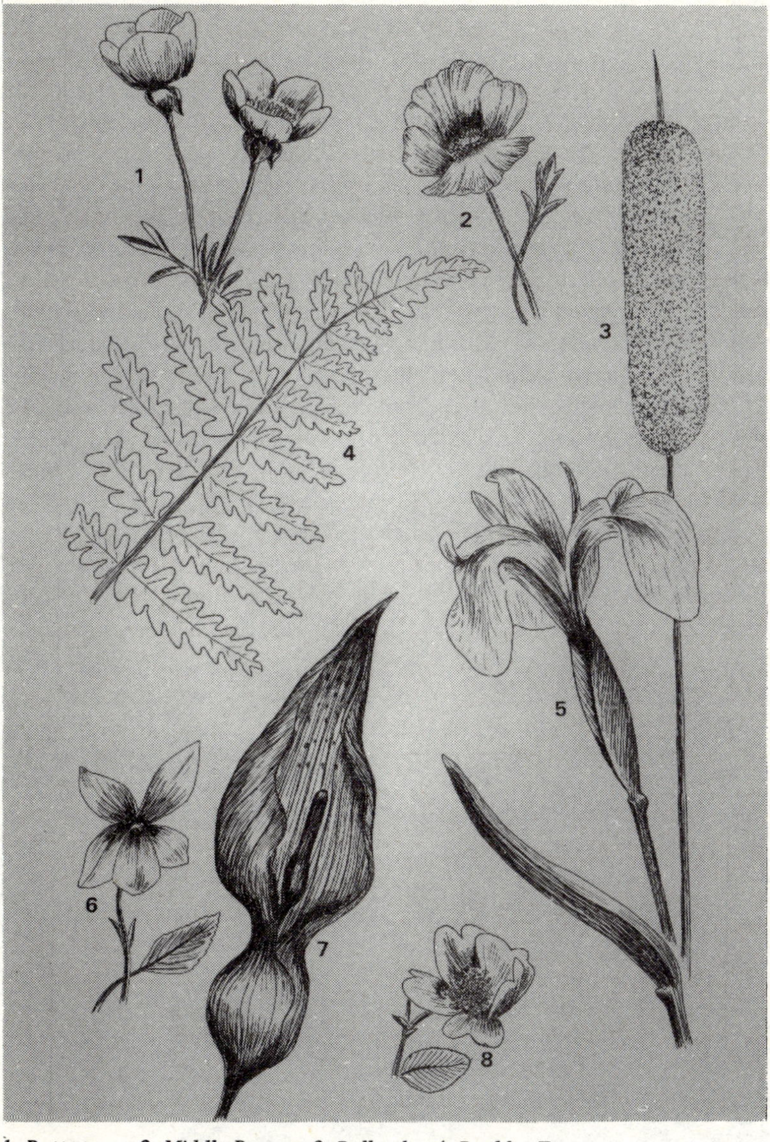

1. Buttercup : 2. Middle Poppy : 3. Bullrush : 4. Buckler Fern :
5. Yellow Flag : 6. Violet : 7. Cuckoo Pint : 8. Dog Rose.

Now you can see why I remarked in the spring section that the beginning of the year is easier on the eye. Two favourites of flower arrangers are now well into growth and these are the teazel and the bullrush or reedmace. The bullrush is particularly interesting in its early development. First the narrow leaves sprout up from the yellowed bents of last year's growth, then when these leaves are about three feet high you will notice amongst them other leaves which appear to swell out at the top. Within a very short time this swelling gets bigger until it bursts open, exposing a pointed growth encased within an almost transparent covering. After a few days this covering splits and withers and you are able to see the unmistakable bullrush. At this stage it is pale green, while growing from the top of its head, as it were, is a spike of an equal length, but of a completely different texture from the velvety lower growth. This spike is often mistaken for the seed-bearing part of the plant which it is not, for the seeds are contained in what will eventually be the familiar brown bullrush head. These are not shed until the following February when the brown casing splits and they burst out in a cloud. The upper growth slowly withers into a mass of fluffiness and then drops off leaving behind a pointed yellow spike which remains on the seed head. Gradually the seed head changes from

Young **Rabbit** **Primrose**

green to a slowly darkening brown, and this is when they are collected for decorative purposes. Should you pick some to brighten your window ledge, beware of handling the heads too much once they have dried, for I write from experience when I say the seeds burst out in a cloud. Ideal for spreading the seeds outside, but less practical when they are sown over carpet and furnishings!

The teazel head at this time is green and within a few weeks will flower into a tight mass of purple blooms set in the midst of small and narrow leaves. By the time winter comes around they will be quite dead, yet still retain the perfect shape which is so attractive in vase arrangements. It is also a great favourite of goldfinches for it provides food for them throughout the winter and they may be seen clinging delicately on the swaying heads as they pluck out the unfallen seeds. Strangely in this ultra modern space age, no machine or manufactured hand tool has yet been invented that can replace the teazel for raising the nap on velour or cashmere. In the woollen industry the type used for this is the *fullers* teasel for it has hooked bracts as opposed to the straight spikes of the common teazel. Both may be found all over Britain, but the fullers naturally shows a higher density in areas where it is cultivated for industrial use.

THE DRAGONFLY AND DAMSELFLY

In early summer, on or around areas where bullrushes flourish, you will see the breathtaking beauty of dragonflies and their smaller relations damselflies. I am often asked if these insects are in danger of dying out because they do not seem as common as they were a number of years ago. Whilst agreeing that their number seem to have reduced, my answer is that, as fossilised remains show, they have been around for 300 million years and I am sure they are quite capable of looking after their own future.

Dragonflies are magnificent insects with powerful flight, capable of reaching speeds of up to sixty miles per hour. There are twenty-seven species in Britain, ranging in size from those with a two-inch wing span to the largest at four and a half inches. All have eyes which cover the top and sides of the head, so they miss very little when hunting for prey, which is any flying insect up to the size of butterflies. Damselflies do not have the same flight speed, nor the large eyes, but they live on a similar diet, though their prey is naturally smaller.

When you see these beautiful adults you are witnessing the final stage in what has been quite a long life, because for almost two years they have lived under water, down in the mud, as ugly larvae or nymphs. Like the adults the larvae are carnivorous, eating anything from the tiniest of insects up to small fish, which are impaled on two hooks protruding from an extension of the lower lip. Drawn into the jaws and sucked dry, their spent, mummified bodies are then left to float off downstream.

The length of this larval stage depends on the availability of food, but however long, eventually the larvae climb up plant stems and out of water. After a short time, perhaps twenty minutes, the skin along the back splits open, and the dragonfly sticks out its head and thorax, then as the sun dries its gauzy wings, they unfold, and after a few practice flutters the fully fledged adult flies off in search of food.

Mating takes place immediately, for their life span in this stage is at the most one month. Some of the species crawl beneath the water to lay their eggs, others lay them on plant stems, while a few actually drop them into the water as they fly over it, many I am afraid into the open mouths of waiting fish.

FERNS

In damp and shady areas ferns are springing up, but as we have well over fifty varieties growing in the British Isles I will not attempt to list them all. Identification is easily made from other plants by the clumps of spores to be seen on the underneath side of the leaves, for ferns are flowerless plants, reproducing not by seed but by spores, in the same way as mushrooms and fungi. The term *fern* normally conjures up in people's minds the tall curling fronds of the bracken, which is the largest – reaching six feet or more – and the most common, but there are ferns as small as one inch. This tiny fern is known as wall-rue; it is quite common and, as its name suggests, grows on walls and rock faces and looks much like a darker version of our vegetable – garden parsley. Fossilized ferns have been found and dated as old as 300 million years, and the prehistoric forbears of today's plants actually formed our earliest forests, and when they died, laid down the foundations of present day coal seams.

These ancient growths were enormous compared with our tallest fern, often reaching in excess of a hundred feet, yet were still the primitive plants that they are today – in fact even now they are among the most primitive on earth.

GRASSES

The most important plants we have both aesthetically and economically are some which grow in every conceivable habitat, yet are probably the most ignored. Dismissed by the amateur naturalist and average rambler as merely a soft carpet to be walked on, a backdrop to fill in the gaps between more interesting plants or something merely to soften the landscape, are the grasses and the sedges.

The economic value of the grasses lies in the fact that apart from the various types that are grown for animal feedstuff in the form of hay and silage, wheat, barley and oats are also encompassed within this order.

By virtue of modifications made over many years, farmers can now grow grasses to suit their own particular locality, and they can also grow various species with a definite end product in mind. For instance, they may want a crop suitable for early grazing or late grazing for their cattle, or they might wish to cut it for hay or for turning into silage. This is grass which is cut while young and green and is stored in a *clamp*, which functions by excluding the air from the grass, thus keeping it fresh and edible for a long period. Sometimes only one species is sown as a break crop or ley, which means that after a field has had a succession of cereals grown in it, the nutrition has been taken from the ground, so a one to three year ley gives the ground a chance to replenish itself. Often five or six types of grass are grown together, so the field you are looking over could very likely contain timothy grass, italian rye, perennial rye, cocksfoot and both the tall and the meadow fescue. In addition to these grasses which are grown to provide valuable supplement to the feed, you could probably see white clover and such herbs as dandelion, yarrow, ribwort, plantain and chicory.

Cattle grazing on the hill opposite my window are controlled by an electric fence, which is moved daily to provide them with a clean, fresh strip of grass. From a distance one cannot see the wire, but only a solid line of cattle, shoulder to shoulder, munching their way gradually across the hill, leaving behind them the pale green of cropped grass, while in front of them there is the darker green of untouched luxuriant growth. Visitors who are not too conversant with farming ways, upon witnessing this spectacle think that the cows are very well drilled.

When people talk of *grass* they generally mean the commonest annual poa and the meadow poa respectively, for these are green throughout the year, never grow very high and are quite uninteresting. Yet many others are most attractive, like the quake grass which is at its best in early summer, although it becomes quite inconspicuous later in the year when overshadowed by taller foliage. This grass has very fine silky stems that quiver and dance in the slightest breeze, and as the heads have alternate bands of green and purple this gives it an iridescent appearance. The tufted hair grass is probably the most beautiful when seen in a clump, for the panicle in which the silvery blooms of the flowers are carried is most delicate, having an almost hair-like fineness so that the drooping foliage when seen from a distance gives the impression of an area of low mist or a faint patch of spray. Yorkshire fog is another grass of silvery appearance and delicate growth which may be found everywhere, particularly in dry places, though it tends not to grow in quite such breathtaking clumps as the tufted.

Sweet vernal deserves its name, for though not outstanding in appearance, it contributes most to that never to be forgotten smell of new-mown hay which is one of the attractions of a British summer. Though slim and inconspicuous it is very hardy and can withstand the most adverse conditions.

There are three types of grass, adding no scenic value to the landscape, which are more important than their unprepossessing appearance would have you suppose, because if they were not there, before very long this very landscape would be gradually eroded away. Townsends cord grass has adapted itself to salt marshes and seashores, where, with its dense underground root system, it stabilizes mud banks from being swept away by the sea. Marram grass and sand couch, both similar in appearance, have adapted themselves to what must be the most inhospitable of terrain – sand dunes – where, like the cord grass, they spread their tough roots and prevent the wind and the sea from slowly wearing away the scenery.

Grass seeds are mainly spread by the wind, but, as an additional method of sowing the seeds over an area as wide as possible, most seeds have a sharp point at one end for the purpose of hooking them into the fur and feathers of animals and birds. If you have ever tried to brush these seeds from woollen stockings or jerseys you will appreciate how effective these points are. What is interesting is that most seeds have the ability to plant themselves. When they are dry they twist in a clockwise direction and when they are wet they twist anti-clockwise and by doing this they bore a hole into the ground. An unfortunate side effect is that should they not fall from the fur they are clinging to they will begin twisting and untwisting until they have buried themselves into the animal's skin, where they cause extreme discomfort. For this reason never ignore a grass seed that might blow into your eye; remove it immediately.

When heavy rainstorms beat flowers to the ground they stay there; equally, if you trampled on them, drove cattle across them, or pulled a heavy roller through their midst they would remain flattened, never to rise again. Have you noticed that this sort of treatment is meted out to grass, yet within a short time it springs back again as though nothing had happened? The reason for this is due to the solid *node* from which the leaves grow. Composed of turgescent material the node's function is to push back the leaf after it has been laid flat. Another example of how the plants protect themselves can be seen in very dry weather. You will notice that the long blade-like leaves roll up, causing many people to imagine that they have withered, though this is not the case. On one side of the leaf there are cells, which trigger off a reaction when a certain level of moisture loss is felt; this reaction causes the leaf to roll up, thereby reducing the area of the leaf exposed to the sun's rays and preventing further loss by evaporation. After a downpour of rain this is why the grass seems to have grown a couple of inches, when really all it has done is to have uncurled.

So much for the grasses, but what about the wildlife which inhabits this underfoot jungle? From a visual point of view, a walk through dense undergrowth might not be too interesting, but certainly the many squeaks, chirps and rustles can give your imagination free rein.

THE COMMON SHREW

Swift rustles followed by piercing, needle-sharp squeaks that make you halt in your tracks and peer hopefully (or fearfully) into the long grass or bracken around your feet, invariably issue from the tiny frame of the common shrew. Being highly strung, restless creatures, they are constantly on the move, racing this way and that through tunnels in the grass, while every now and then they burst into vociferous piping screams, as they happen across intruders into their territory, for their chosen patch is hallowed ground to be guarded with jealous aggression.

If you keep perfectly still after hearing these high pitched squeaks, you will stand a very good chance of observing the shrew without it being aware of your presence, and if you should happen to have your feet on one of its runways, it will clamber over them without a moment's hesitation. If you get a close look at one, you might imagine that by virtue of its bright beadlike eyes set at the base of a long, mobile snout, it has excellent eyesight. Indeed, it certainly gives the impression of extreme vigilance, but in fact it is notoriously weak sighted, and depends almost entirely on its sense of smell. Strangely, it does not seem too perturbed by the presence of a human scent, but a wrong move will send it streaking away in a flash.

The shrew's very prominent snout makes an easy field identification between it and any other rodent with which it might be confused. However, although mouselike in appearance and habit, the shrew is not classed as a mouse but grouped within an order of insect eaters, or insectivora, to which the mole and the hedgehog belong. Until one has studied the habits of these three and found many close resemblances, this classification must seem as diverse as grouping together the bearlike badger with the tiny weasel, and the water-loving otter with the tree-climbing marten, yet these four, along with the stoat and polecat, are related in the family known as mustelidae.

At this time of the year a most amusing sight is the mother shrew leading her brood around in a similar manner to that of elephants, each tiny shrew holding the tail of the one in front. However the difference between shrews and elephants is that shrews carry out this *follow my leader* at high speed, so that often those at the end of the line are literally swept off their feet, while still grimly hanging on to the tail in front.

Situated at the base of the tail, in common with many other mammals, the shrew has scent glands which are used for marking out their territory, and for leaving signposts and trails to locate each other. A point often quoted is that these scent glands act as a defence mechanism because of the vile taste and smell they produce. Admittedly, many carnivores would not dream of actually eating a shrew, but there are a few exceptions such as birds of prey and some of the larger fish, who snap up the shrew when it is taking a swim, which it does often just for pleasure. On the other hand, most flesh eaters do not hesitate for a moment before *killing* one, so to be killed but not eaten hardly qualifies these glands as a successful means of protection.

Shrews are completely harmless to man and are actually beneficial because of their destruction of many field and garden pests. Insects make up a great part of their diet, supplemented by slugs, caterpillars, small fish, frogs and other aquatic creatures. That they consume great quantities of earthworms is not to their credit, but I suppose we must accept their bad faults as well as their good.

Dead shrews are a common sight in the countryside. Discounting those carcasses to be found on our roads, there are more corpses of shrews than of any other animal. There can be many reasons for this, because their normal life expectancy is not very long, normally fourteen months at the most. Coupled with this fact, their nervous system is very delicately balanced, so although they are very aggressive to their own kind, fighting ferociously when necessary, the slightest unexpected shock can kill them. However, I would think that starvation plays a strong role in decimating them because it could be said of shrews that they eat to live, and live to eat. For every thirty-six hours they must consume two ounces of food and if they cannot find a meal, or are prevented from eating for three or four hours, they die. As a result of this voracious appetite they have alternately to eat and sleep throughout the day and night.

I have written of the common shrew, which is widespread throughout the British mainland, yet another of this species more deserving of the title *common* is the pygmy shrew, for this shrew is more often to be seen than any other. Two inches in body length, it is one inch smaller than the common shrew, but in all other respects is identical. The remaining three species are very localised and are not likely to be found by the casual rambler.

TURN OVER THAT STONE

When I am out walking, I can never pass a large stone, small fallen tree or, for that matter, any object that might harbour life of some sort, without turning it over. There is a great deal of excitement in not knowing what will be exposed. And although throughout the year something may be discovered, summer-time is when the most interesting creatures appear, transfixed by the sudden blinding light as their cover is suddenly lifted.

REPTILES

This time of the year is the only time to see any of our snake families, although if the weather is particularly warm there is a great likelihood that they might be found on top of stones rather than underneath them.

In the evolutionary scale the niche left between amphibeans, such as frogs and newts, and birds and mammals, is filled by a very large group of animals known as reptiles. Throughout the world we have something in the region of six thousand species contained within this classification; almost half of these are snakes, while the remainder are crocodiles and related families, turtles, tortoises and lizards. Yet despite these vast numbers, the species of reptiles we have in this country number only six – three snakes and three lizards.

Common Lizard

LIZARDS

As with most of our rarer wildlife, whether bird, mammal or insect, luck plays a great part in any sighting and this is the case with the sand lizard, a comparative rarity today. Apart from being rare, it is at the same time restricted to localized areas of southern England – which are the New Forest in Hampshire, areas of Dorset and Surrey and along the coasts of Cheshire and Lancashire. This lizard's name does not mean that it may only be found in areas of sand, for it also likes dry, woodland places and heaths as well as sand dunes. Whilst the adult sand lizard is an average length of eight inches compared with the six inches of the common lizard, before you pen your rare discovery to the local paper it would be best to check the colouration carefully, because the common lizard has also been known to reach these proportions.

At a glance the two species are similar, but the former has a tendency to shade into green all the year round, and this is even more pronounced in the early summer mating season.

As to habits, both lead similar lives, but as you are most likely to see the common lizard, I will refer to that. Beautifully camouflaged they are almost undetectable in the undergrowth, though on sunny days you cannot help but be aware of their fleeting movements in the grass for like the tiny shrew they are guaranteed to arrest your attention, forcing you to search the scant grasses or probe wildly with a stick, eventually to find nothing at all, for they have a habit of appearing to vanish into thin air. Even when flushed out from their hiding places they hardly pause to accustom their eyes to the sudden brightness before streaking away. When they do venture out onto ground which contrasts with their own colour, they may be studied with ease, for such time as you can remain immobile.

The principal food of lizards comprises of beetles, moths and flies. Spiders, too, are eaten, and while small caterpillars are swallowed whole, larger types are chewed, the tough skins being rejected. This selective method also applies to crickets and grasshoppers.

All species of lizards have the ability to allow part, or all, of their tail to be broken off, and this drastic step is used to effect an escape should the tail be gripped. Technically this is known as *autotomy*. Whilst the unfortunate lizard must suffer a certain amount of inconvenience no pain is caused, for this lesion is in no way similar to a leg being torn off. That Nature designed the tail to break off easily is fascinating. This is how it takes place. The vertebrae, or small bones making up the tail, have a pre-formed hairline crack across the centre. Upon dislocation of the tail, scales on the skin are pulled apart, the skin underneath is broken and the surrounding muscles are pulled out of sheaths, which then allow the vertebrae to separate. Nature also had the forethought to supply lizards with the ability to regrow a new tail, or if the need arose a second or third tail. Though even if these new tails are functional, they never look the same as the original, tending to be rather stumpy. Should you ever attempt to catch a lizard, give a thought to its pride or vanity, and make sure you always pick it up by the shoulders.

The female common lizard retains her eggs inside her body right up until the moment of birth, then when oviposition takes place these eggs are broken and the young ones, numbering from six to ten, are dropped wherever she might be. As no hatching is needed no nest is required either. Once born, the mother has no further interest in her babies' welfare so they remain where they were born for several days without moving. Eventually hunger forces them to begin hunting for small insects such as the soft bodied aphids, for their partially developed teeth are not capable of tackling any tougher food.

The sand lizard lays her eggs in a hole in the soil, which she covers, leaving actual incubation to the warmth of the sun. Laid in July, if the weather is suitable, the eggs hatch out during August.

The third of our lizards I have deliberately left to last, because this one is more often thought of as a snake than a lizard. But the slow worm or blind worm, although having characteristics of both, is definitely a lizard without legs. It is certainly no relation of the worm, and if you have ever tried to catch one you will appreciate that it is anything but slow. Possibly the name was given to it by early naturalists who observed that it was neither snake nor lizard and so chose worm as a happy medium – while as it sheds its skin in common with other reptiles, the term for this being *to slough*, it was prefixed *slough worm* and this was eventually corrupted to *slow*. At the same time, though its eyes are very small, it is by no means blind, having sight equally as good as other reptiles.

Once you have handled a slow worm it should dispel for ever the myth that reptiles are slimy creatures, for the skin is dry and has a very smooth, shiny texture which feels like vinyl to the touch. So smooth is this skin that the slow worm can slip through your fingers with ease, making it very difficult to hold.

Adults range in size from a pencil-slim six inches to a thumb-thick eighteen inches in length. Their colouring, too, can show wide variation, appearing from very dark brown to bright yellow, depending a great deal on the age of the specimen; for the older it gets the darker it becomes. Females have a dark line running down the middle of the back and both sexes often have pale blue spots irregularly scattered over the body.

Slow worms may be found throughout Great Britain but a higher incidence is concentrated in the warmer south. Their diet is the same as that of other lizards but in addition they consume great quantities of worms and slugs. They gorge themselves to repletion on the small greyish white slug that is such a nuisance to gardeners. As this delicious morsel tends to be nocturnal this is when the slow worm is most active. Sadly, many hundreds of slow worms are needlessly killed every year by gardeners who are ignorant of the good they can do.

SNAKES

Of our three species of snakes, the smooth snake is particularly rare; few sightings are made of it each year and then only in some southern counties. As a guide to identification, should you be fortunate enough to come across one, they grow to some twenty inches in length and their colour varies from grey to chestnut. On each side and top of the head there is a dark patch, while down the back runs a column of dark spots. The smooth snake will bite if picked up but without poisoning.

The grass snake is green or olive brown with vertical black markings along the flanks. This snake is also harmless, although it is able to frighten the uninitiated by putting on a great show of hissing and thrashing. It would, however, be unusual to see a grass snake in this state, for being highly sensitive to the slightest ground vibration it usually disappears from sight before you can get too close. However, when they are basking above the ground, on a rock for example, it is sometimes possible to creep quite near. Usually they are to be found

near water and it is not uncommon to see them swimming, for apart from slugs, slow worms and small rodents, they prey quite heavily on frogs, newts and small fishes. In the nesting season they take eggs and fledglings and many egg collectors have had palpitations after grasping a wriggling snake which had curled up for a sleep in the nest from which it had just despatched the contents.

Less frequently seen than the grass snake, yet certainly more common, is the adder, or viper as it is known in the north. This snake should be given a wide berth, as should all the snakes if you are not too sure which is which. The darting tongue of the adder, as with other harmless snakes and lizards, has nothing to do with its poisoning capabilities, for it is simply an organ through which they can scent out and follow their prey. The needle sharp fangs which are actually hollow teeth connected to a reservoir of poisonous venom, are hinged so that when they are not in use they may be folded flat along the roof of the mouth. This venom, while causing the rapid death of small prey, such as rats and rabbits, is rarely fatal to humans and there have only been ten deaths recorded in the past fifty years in this country. However, death is possible for the poison is a heart depressant and the people whom it would be most likely to affect would be the very young or the very old. Gamekeepers and anyone who works on the land stand a greater chance than the average person of coming into contact with adders, and often carry ampoules of snake-bite serum, although by law only a doctor is allowed to administer it.

The colour of the adder is basically yellow or pale brown, but the most distinctive feature is a wide, dark coloured zig-zag pattern down the centre of the back. On the upper surface of the head there is also a prominent V-shaped mark.

No snakes of any species are to be found wild in Ireland, and for this omission legend has it that thanks (or black marks if you are an Irish naturalist) should be given to St Patrick who banished them from the country. The adder is reasonably common in all other parts of Great Britain, and in Scotland it is more prominent than any other species.

Top: **Common Lizard**
Centre: **Adder**
Bottom: **Grass Snake**

HIDDEN INSECTS

Apart from small mammals and interesting reptiles, stone turning can also throw light on a host of fascinating insect life. Some of the more spectacular varieties are worthy of note.

Millipedes and centipedes are probably the most commonly found, though these names are really terms for a species rather than for two individual insects. Under the nomenclature *millipede* are embraced some seventy-nine different types, while the label *centipede* incorporates seventy-one kinds, many of these quite rare. Those centipedes normally found under the same stone or log are the swift-moving, red-coloured variety, typical of what one imagines this species to look like, and the slower moving, but similarly coloured *stone dweller* – which has legs a great deal longer and moves like an animated hair brush. Their opposite numbers are respectively, the yellow-tinted snake millipede and the smaller flat millipede. The difference between these separate species is that centipedes have one pair of legs on each segment, while millipede have two pairs. Actually both seem to disregard the number of legs they are supposed to have by virtue of the prefixes *centi* and *milli* for their legs are governed by how many segments they have, so the largest can have a total of one hundred and eighty legs, while the smallest may have only forty. By the way, centipedes bite, millipedes do not, so if you are unsure of the difference don't pick one up.

The pill millipede is often confused with the wood louse, for it is similarly segmented and has a habit of curling up into a tight ball when disturbed. This insect is a shiny black in colour and when curled up does look like a perfectly round pill.

The wood louse, though living under the same stone, is in no way related. At the same time it is not a louse at all, nor has it any affinity for wood other than to live under it. Surprisingly, for a complete land lover, it is a crustacean, closely related to crabs, prawns and shrimps.

Of the many beetles which may be discovered, one in particular can be a little frightening, for it puts on quite an aggressive display when alarmed. Better known by name than sight, the devil's coach horse is one and a quarter inches long and a dull grey-black in colour. Its most conspicuous feature is its frontal pincers which, when spread wide apart, are considerably greater than the width of the body and very capable of giving a painful bite. When disturbed, it immediately raises itself on its forelegs and cocks its tail in the manner of a scorpion or earwig, and opens wide its jaws – a veritable dragon of the undergrowth. At this point many people fearfully react by pounding the beetle insensible with the stone they have raised, or else they stamp it into oblivion. Yet had they known something of its dietary habits they would have allowed it to resume its business, for, by feeding on enormous quantities of injurious vegetable pests, it is a great friend of both gardener and farmer alike. However, until the devil's coach horse learns something of human nature, then alters its appearance to something more attractive and colourful, I am afraid it will have to suffer the continuous persecution which, as the name suggests, has been carried out since the superstition-ridden Dark Ages.

Some other friends of man are more likely to be found by those who are not of a squeamish nature, for they may be observed carrying out their good work under or around the corpses of dead animals. These are the undertakers of nature, the burying or sexton beetles.

The ripe smell of decomposing flesh attracts these beetles from a considerable distance and they immediately fly in and proceed with their traditional chore. Not, I hasten to add, from any sense of public hygiene, but purely to provide somewhere to lay their eggs.

It is the male of the species which picks up the scent of carrion, and once it has zoned into the source, it will give out a scent of its own making which in turn attracts the female from as much as half a mile away. If the ground underneath the corpse is too hard or stony for them to dig into they slowly drag it, inch by inch, to a more suitable position. Should it be too large for them to move they will even go so far as to remove portions of the dead creature to lighten the load. The same treatment is given to any legs or wings which have become snagged on branches or rocks. Naturally they will only attempt to move animals up to the size of blackbirds or rats; anything larger which could not be buried would be abandoned.

Satisfied with the site, up to three pairs of beetles begin to scrape away the surrounding earth and, by burrowing underneath, remove the soil until the corpse gradually sinks into the ensuing pit. By working continuously this mammoth task, surprisingly, does not take very long, and soon the body of the animal or bird is conveniently below the level of the soil. Now the female lays her eggs around or in crevices of the carcass, then she covers over the grave with soil that she had previously heaped up around it.

When the sluggish, grey-black larvae hatch from the eggs, they are well provided with food, so naturally they spend their whole larval period within this gruesome larder. However, when the next stage of their life approaches – pupation – they dig away from the now skeletal corpse, to form a small earthen cell, in which their metamorphosis takes place, and then as adults they are ready to carry out similar searches for carrion.

Of the seven species we have of this type of beetle, they are for the most part jet-black and marked with orange, red or yellow bands so you should not be in too much doubt when you do discover them. The exception is the largest of the family, which grows up to one and a half inches in length as opposed to the normal three quarters of an inch of the others. This type lacks the warning colouration, for as it is a night flyer, there is no need to be anything other than completely black.

The peeling bark of rotten trees invariably hides a multitude of insect fauna. The best known beetle, but one that does not seem as numerous as it used to be, is the stag beetle, familiar because of its large size and the fearsome pincers worn by the male. Actually the reason for these antler-like horns is not clear, for due to the weakness of the muscles controlling them they are quite useless as weapons, and if you were to put your finger between them you would only feel the slightest of pressure. Yet how many people dare? Obviously they exist as a visual deterrent. Apart from the jaws, the female is similar in appearance, having the same dull black colouring. After mating she burrows into a rotten tree stump to lay her eggs, which soon hatch out into fat white grubs. By peeling away the decayed wood you can often expose these larvae, which are quite spectacular, in most cases being as long, and as thick, or thicker, than a man's finger. They have a very long development period taking in excess of three years before reaching adulthood. Adults fly strongly and very noisily sounding almost like a small electric motor as they pass overhead on a still summer's evening, and it takes very strong nerves indeed not to run screaming through the woods when male or female inadvertently alights on you, or drops silently onto your head as you pass under the tree.

Stag beetles are normally only found in England, but so that the

Scots would not feel slighted, Nature gave them a wood boring beetle exclusive to their pine forests. Three quarters of an inch long and dull brown, the timberman, as it is appropriately known, would be quite ordinary if it were not for its antennae which, at three inches, are the longest of any of our beetles. These extended antennae are the trade mark of a group of beetles known as longhorns, though none of the other sixty-nine species have antennae that reach the length of those of the timberman.

The finest specimen of our longhorns, common everywhere, is the musk beetle, so-named because it is able to exude a very strong musky scent. It may be found in rotten willow trees, and its general form is about an inch long, quite narrow and parallel sided. Its beauty lies in its colouration, for the wing cases, or elytra, are a sparkling metallic greenish-bronze, while the thorax is a deep shade of chestnut. The larvae of this beetle live in willow wood and are off-white, slightly flattened grubs. Typical of most wood borers they are armed with powerful jaws which enable them to munch their way through the trees. Also typical is the fact that they take a number of years to mature.

The wasp beetle is very common and may be seen flying in the summer sunshine or running about on fence posts or trees. The fact that this insect is black with yellow lines interlacing its body was enough for early naturalists to prefix it with the name *wasp,* but it bears no other resemblance to a wasp, although it possibly gains some protection from the real wasp's notoriety.

Another tiny beetle is worth mentioning and this is the notorious elm bark beetle. The end product of this creature's work is possibly better known to most people than the beetle itself, for it is largely responsible for the Dutch elm disease that has hit the headlines over the past couple of years and caused thousands of trees to be felled. The elm bark beetle is a short thick-set chestnut coloured insect and may be found by peeling back the bark of elms which have been cut down and left on the ground, or by examination of those elms which show obvious signs of decay. Often, if the tree is still standing and has lost none of its bark, the presence of this insect will be given away by piles of reddish dust at the base made by the adults as they bore their way out of the bark.

What is interesting about the species known as bark beetles, of which the elm bark beetle is just one of many, is that each type has its own pattern for burrowing behind the bark. Once you have learned the plan for each individual, identification may be made without ever setting eyes on the culprit. Should you wish to make a study of these fascinating insects you will gain your basic knowledge from books which deal with this subject in depth, but as an example I will give you some idea of what to expect from the elm bark beetle.

First, the female bores a hole through the thick bark until she reaches the cambium tissue, then, dropping an egg at short intervals as she goes, she channels out a vertical groove sometimes as long as two feet. When the resultant larvae hatch out they, too, begin to tunnel, but they branch off at right angles to the main gallery. You will see this fascinating pattern once you have pulled back the bark, and you will also observe that each of as many as fifty grooves gradually grows wider in diameter as it projects away from the parent groove. This is because the larvae is growing with every step it takes. I have stated groove here and not tunnel, for you will see the corresponding half is in the bark you have peeled away. When fully grown the larvae makes a small chamber in which to pupate and having done this, it then bores straight out through the bark to fly to another elm to continue the cycle, very likely carrying with it the fungus that causes Dutch elm disease.

WOODPECKERS

We have some allies in the fight to eradicate bark boring pests even though they are hopelessly outnumbered. Their interest though, is purely selfish, for to woodpeckers, bark beetles are a much enjoyed delicacy.

We have three resident species of woodpecker in Great Britain and one summer visitor, which is the wry neck. Again the south seems to have monopolised these very pretty and interesting birds for only the greater spotted is numerous in Scotland and none at all may be found in Ireland, though ornithologists have recorded an increase of the green woodpecker in northern areas.

The resonant, vibrating *tap tap tap* that carries for great distances on the balmy summer air, rarely means that a woodpecker is chiselling out its supper, or that it is boring out a nesting hole, but simply that it is drumming out a warning to other woodpeckers to keep out of its chosen terrain. It is no accident that this sound is so far reaching, for the woodpecker deliberately chooses a log or branch that is sufficiently hollow and dry to produce a ringing tone. While pursuing food in the form of grubs and beetles hiding behind bark, the sound is somewhat muted, for the wood is invariably soft and partially decayed.

The green woodpecker, at twelve inches in length, is the largest and most common, but due to the green camouflaging colour of its upper body it is not easy to catch sight of when perched on the bole of a tree. If the light within the wood is not favourable for identification, its method of flight should be enough, for it progresses in what can best be described as a series of aerial bounds, by flapping its rather short wings only on the up-glide. Having settled on the vertical plane of a tree trunk, where it clings as comfortably as a fly on a wall, it proceeds upwards, sideways or round and round the trunk in a series of short jerks. Every few hops it pauses, holding its head well back while listening for the tiny sounds from behind the bark which mean that an unsuspecting grub is chewing its way towards extinction. Having located such a morsel, the woodpecker drills into the bark with unerring aim, its head moving with eye-blurring rapidity, as its pneumatic beak goes to work. Should the grub be situated deep in the tree, the bird has a trump card, as nature has provided it with a tongue, attached to the skull with elastic tissue, capable of stretching out to four times the length of its beak, which means it can reach to the bottom of small holes that are in excess of six inches deep. As an added assistance, the tongue is serrated, and covered in a sticky substance.

Apart from their main diet of wood insects, woodpeckers have a liking for ants. On grassy hillsides, where the meadow ants throw up their mounds, or in fir woods where the wood ant builds its great cities. you may come across the aftermath of a woodpecker's meal where the nests are torn away, leaving scattered masses of grass, earth and pine needles spread over a wide area. On rare occasions, they make surreptitious forays into quiet country gardens, where they dig great holes in well-kept lawns, in search of grass. Even the keenest gardener could not fail to cherish the sight of such an exotic visitor albeit at the expense of his *billiard table.*

The greater and lesser spotted woodpeckers are also known as the pied and barred woodpeckers respectively. Both are black and white birds, although each has contrasts of buff brown, blackish brown and crimson markings on its head. Yet despite this very bold colour scheme they are more difficult to see than the green woodpecker, for in the dappled patterns of light and shade to be found in woodlands, they become virtually invisible and it is only when they are out in the open, perched on a telegraph pole or fence, that you will be able to appreciate their beautiful feathers.

The greater is nine inches long and the lesser is just under six inches, but while there is a difference in size and colour, the basic habits and diet of these and the green woodpecker are identical. It should be noted that no woodpecker ever drills holes in healthy trees, so in this respect they do no disservice to man; in fact exactly the opposite, for when they do begin to bore it is a sure sign that beetles or weevils are already at work. When the forester notices this he may have a chance either to treat the tree or weed it out and prevent infestation to other trees.

The wry neck woodpecker, our summer visitor, is related to, and similar in many respects, to the other three, although it does lack the very bold patterns of their dress. It does not bore into trees however, but jerks all over the trunk picking its food from the surface of the bark, giving the mistaken impression that it is pecking holes. Orchards are the most likely situations to watch out for this bird, though due to this preference they suffered heavy losses through insecticide poisoning, so are not common enough to be seen very often, which is a great pity. The name wry neck is well earned for it has the ability to swivel its head round in an almost complete circle, as if its neck consisted of a ball and socket joint.

None of these four has a song as such but nevertheless they have their distinctive calls. The greater and the lesser content themselves with an abrupt *tchick tchick,* the wry neck gives a loud rapid *quee quee quee,* while the green, an obvious extrovert, gives a raucous, ringing peal of laughter (no other word describes it) which has earned it the nickname of *yaffle.* If you have not heard these cries by the end of May, you will have to wait until the following year as their noisy passage ends rather abruptly.

WANING BIRDSONG

This halting of bird-song is general, yet many people, being unaware of the crescendo reached in spring, are by the same token incognisant that there is a tapering off as the year progresses. This begins in June, when the diminution of song is noticeable, for with families to rear, most species, worn by parental cares, have neither the time nor inclination to express their feelings. By July and August a great silence has descended upon hedgerows and woods, broken only by a few exceptions, the robin being the most conspicuous of these. This virtual silence is due to the moulting season, a time when perhaps because their change of feathers is uncomfortable their rather scruffy state makes them feel depressed, or that the physical effort of regenerating new clothing whilst feeding insatiable youngsters knocks the spirit out of them. Whatever the reason, no joyful trilling is forthcoming.

Out in the open fields there is rather more song, but nothing to compare with that of the preceding months. Yellowhammers, corn, and reed buntings still sing, but their efforts are short-lived and rather lifeless. Disturb a reed bed by day or night and you may get an answering burst of song from a sedge-warbler, short in duration and somewhat querulous, but in the main most avian songsters are reluctant to give voice. Towards the end of August a few species begin practising their autumn chorus – subdued echoes of springtime, but buoyant bird-song proper ends in July.

SWALLOWS

Four birds who are invariably lumped together under the one title of *swallow* are to me the very epitome of summer, in the same way that the cuckoo is the essence of springtime. These are the house martin, sand martin, swift and the swallow proper.

To differentiate between the species is to many people as difficult as separating rook, jackdaw and crow, yet with these and the swallow types, a little knowledge and mild observation goes a long way towards making identification very simple.

Nesting habits play a large part in ease of identification. For while many books suggest that you can differentiate between a swift and a swallow by the fact that the former has a tiny white spot under its chin, you would need telescopic eyesight to see this mark, for they wheel and gyrate at speeds up to sixty miles an hour.

The sand martin is easy to identify, for whilst flying with the other species it is noticeably the smallest, and when it returns home it is to the sandy cliffs, steep railway cuttings and other vertical planes where the earth is suitable for excavating burrows. None of the other species nest in such situations. These burrows, which the birds dig out themselves, are normally from one to two feet in depth and fairly high so as to be out of reach. The nest itself is simply a mass of dried grasses and feathers onto which four or five pinkish-white eggs are laid in May. Being the first to arrive in this country by a short head, and having no nest to build as such, their eggs are laid much sooner than the others. Whether these nests in holes are particularly conducive to insect life I am not sure, but the last time I put my arm into one, in a sandy quarry in Hertfordshire, I found afterwards that I was host to a horrifying number of bird fleas. If your main interest lies in bird parasites then you now know what to do, but I must confess that insect study was furthest from my mind as I frantically searched them out.

The swift, swallow and house martin are all birds with a close affinity for the buildings of man, but all to varying degrees. The house martin is responsible for those cup-like structures, formed completely of tiny pats of mud, which cling firmly to the fascias and gable ends of houses. Apart from this exclusive habit, its underparts are completely snow-white, separating it from the swallow, which has a very visible red chin and the swift which is grey-black all over apart from the aforementioned white spot under the chin.

Swallows construct an open topped nest, again with globules of mud which they stick on top of projecting beams, rafters and purlins *inside* buildings. Occasionally they will take over from, or build a nest close to, the martins. The swifts, too, favour nesting sites within buildings and roofs, but their nests are only ramshackle affairs of grass and feathers glued together with saliva.

Actually martins may be used as barometers of pending rain or continued fine weather. While they fly high in the sky there is no fear of sudden showers, but when they skim low along the ground don't plan a picnic tea on the lawn unless you envisage wearing gum boots and waterproof coat. The reason is simple and in no way due to prophetic insight. When the air is damp and rain approaches, though this may not be apparent to us, flying insects and particularly midges stay close to the ground, so this is naturally where they are hotly pursued and swiftly snapped up by the very large mouths of the martins. Butterflies, beetles and, in the evenings, large moths are also taken in mid-flight, and with breathtaking accuracy insects will be plucked daintily from wall-tops, swept from grass heads and even skimmed from the surface of water. They seem to live most of their lives on the wing, even to the extent of drinking by taking in mouthfuls of water as they splash across the surface of a pond or stream. They resemble bats in the half light of approaching dusk having a similar jerky undulating flight pattern, also drinking from gutters while treading air.

The gentle twittering song or cry of the swallow and martin intermingled with the piercing scream of the swift, as it swings around the house, become part of everyday sounds. Beginning early in the morning and continuing throughout the day until darkness falls, their sounds become so much a part of the scene that it is not until they disappear at the beginning of September that you realise what a beautiful addition they were to a summer's day – almost, one could say, the background music of the season.

Out in the fields and open moorlands it is the sky lark who adds this musical background, for who can remain unmoved by the sound of this tiny brown bird, trilling loudly as it ascends high in the sky until it is a mere speck in the blue. Incidentally this almost non-stop chorus has a practical reason rather than being merely an expression of joy. Being ground birds they fly above their chosen territory and mark out a *vocal boundary,* warning others to keep out, whilst at the same time the song attracts the opposite sex.

Towards the end of August autumnal flocking begins, as our summer visitors prepare to leave, and at the same time those which are with us all the year round congregate together in readiness for the coming winter. This behaviour is brought about by the gradual shortening of the days, which triggers off a chemical reaction within the bird. It has nothing to do with changes in the weather. In the weeks preceding their emigration, birds feed much more actively than normal, so that quite often they double their body weight as they store up fat for the long journey ahead.

This flocking together can be a most impressive sight, as the various species mass together in their thousands, small groups of them gradually flying into an area to join the larger mass who have perhaps taken over a whole strip of woodland. House sparrows desert the places of their name and descend in great bands into the harvest fields, where the resultant damage they do can be measured in thousands of pounds. Starlings, pigeons and lapwings gradually draw together in their separate groups and great clouds of finches momentarily blacken the sky. So in no time at all the whole pattern of summer bird-life changes from bustling activity spread all over the countryside to pockets of noisy excitement, the birds appearing like children waiting in a railway station for the train to take them to the seaside. The sudden exodus is less noticeable in the south, for over a period no sooner does one think they have gone than they appear to have returned – the reason for this is that their place has been taken by flocks moving down from the north. There does not seem to be any apparent segregation of the different species, for quite often one can see mixed flocks taking off. Many species do not group together but fly off individually, the ever solitary cuckoo being a prime example of this.

THE BADGER

For the casual observer, birds are the most abundant wildlife, and ornithology is probably the most popular of country lovers' pursuits. Yet with less effort than many books would lead you to believe, you can catch more than a glimpse of our mammals, and because they are so rarely seen the sighting of them is that much more exciting.

Take the badger. The average person would not dream of attempting to observe this shy and elusive creature, because they have read so often how futile it would be unless they were possessed of the patience and woodcraft skills of a Pawnee Indian. Yet strangely enough the badger is far easier to watch than the fox, which is supposed to be less reserved about human company. Clearly one must make a sensible approach,

The **Badger** *is normally placid, but when the need arises can be a ferocious fighter.*

bearing in mind the fact that animals have a highly developed sense of smell.

First of all, to avoid a fruitless effort, you should find out whether badgers are known to live in your area. There will probably be at least one pair, for they are more widespread than is imagined throughout England, Wales and Ireland and to a slightly lesser degree, Scotland. There are various ways of finding this out, perhaps the easiest being to enquire of someone with local knowledge, for badgers as a rule prefer to colonise the same sett or setts within a small area, for generation after generation.

It would be rare to find setts in very flat country, though even the most featureless planes usually have old, steep-sided river beds or very deep boundary ditches. For badgers always choose a home site on a slope. One reason for this is that digging is made easier for them, and secondly they never risk the chance of being flooded. Dense undergrowth either around or close to the entrance hole is also a must.

Holes in the ground abound everywhere and it takes no skill in finding them, the difficulty only arises when you have to decide whether or not they are occupied, and if so, by what species of animal. Rabbit burrow entrances do not always have the small hole one would expect, but whatever the size, the run up to the entrance is usually strewn with fresh earth and many droppings, and from within you can smell the not unpleasant *rabbity* scent. Foxes' earths, on the other hand, have a very strong scent of urine, although this is not always a guarantee that the *earth* is occupied, for foxes, unlike the badger, change their homes at the slightest whim, except in the period leading up to the birth of cubs and for about six weeks afterwards. At this time although the cubs are not ready to leave her the vixen will move them to a fresh earth, often only a matter of a few hundred yards away.

Unfortunately badgers do not read books, for if they did they would realize that they are supposed to dig out great claw marks in the trees surrounding their setts, leave signposts of dropped bedding straw pointing to their entrances and place latrine holes in full view of passers-by, all as markers that *Brock* is at home. Sometimes these signs may be found, but not nearly as often as the experts would have us believe. Badgers have no distinguishing scent, but to find out if the hole is occupied, and indeed if it is that of a badger and not a temporary fox's earth, the method is simple. If you place a twig across the entrance and bed one end into the soil so that the wind cannot dislodge it, on the following day you will be able to see whether or not any animal has entered, for if they have the twig will have been knocked flat. Make this test on three or four consecutive occasions to make sure that the first was no accident. To find out whether the tenant is a fox or badger, find a well thorned bramble or blackthorn twig and bed it as firmly as you can, two-thirds of the way up the entrance hole, then with a bit of luck you will find on a return visit two or three hairs snagged on the thorns, as an infallible clue.

Once the groundwork is laid, the rest is simple particularly in the early summer months when the cubs are tied to the home sett. If it is the young badgers you wish to see, forget the nocturnal badger and get into a well disguised position at sunrise or in the late afternoon while the sun is still warm. If it is cold or damp, they will not venture out.

A method I have used with considerable success is baiting out within the vicinity of a sett. Most scraps seem to be acceptable, but I find a large knuckle bone works best for two reasons. First, this seems to be a much favoured delicacy, but second and more important, as the bone is large and solid it can be secured firmly in one place and this ensures a good look at *Brock* at table. Once a badger has accepted your food, he will return for it again and again. The same method may be used for the fox.

Built like a bear, related to the stoat, the ponderous, dawn-coated badger is placid by nature and temperament and will usually go out of its way to avoid trouble. Yet should the need arise it will become a ferocious fighting machine which few can equal. Should it be gripped from the rear, by man or animal, the lack of collar bones enables it to twist within its skin and so round on the attacker. An interesting, but daunting, feature is the articulation of the badger's lower jaw. For once closed upon a wrist or ankle, it locks in such a way that dislocation is impossible, and the power is such that a limb could be bitten clean through. Repeated blows about the head would be a waste of time, for down the centre of its skull is a very pronounced ridge which provides solid protection. But like the bear which it resembles, a blow on the nose could kill, the nasal area being unprotected and quite fragile.

To the consternation of fox hunters, should they place their terriers in a fox's earth which also contains a badger – a situation which is by no means rare – mutilation and often death is the fate for their dogs. Squeezing into the furthermost chamber to protect his flanks and rear, *Bawsen* fights with a desperate courage equalled only by that of his attackers. The cunning fox invariably gets behind the badger, within the labyrinth of tunnels, and bolts at the first opportunity.

It is now illegal to kill badgers unless it can be proved that such a course is necessary, though no doubt this will still happen, as it always has in the past. I have known men who have killed them while in the pursuit of foxes simply because the badgers happened to be there. And while badger steaks are regarded as a very fair meal by old, and not so old, countrymen, this aimless destruction will continue.

Often considered to be completely harmless, this is not strictly true, for apart from being just as much a pest as the fox can be when it comes to the slaughter of young game birds, there has been much heated discussion in the farming press as to whether or not badgers are carriers of bovine tuberculosis. Of fifty badger carcasses examined by the Ministry of Agriculture, one was found to be infected with TB, although other sources state that these carcass samples were taken from an area where there was little or no history of TB in cattle herds. On the other hand, among seventy carcasses which were examined in Cornwall where cattle have suffered heavily from this disease, twenty-seven were found to be infected. This indicates that the geographical location of the area in which infected badgers have been found, relates precisely to the area in which new infections amongst herds have occurred.

This is a very emotive subject, with conservationists on one hand and those who are economically affected on the other. One farmer has been quoted as saying 'we cannot afford the luxury of badgers', while another suggests exterminating them completely. Whilst there seems to be no doubt that badgers, along with other forms of wildlife, do spread many diseases, one can only hope that such drastic steps will never be necessary.

I mentioned in my section on spring, how badgers dig out young rabbits from the breeding stops to kill and eat them, yet on many occasions it has been found that rabbits will share a home with badgers and live in perfect harmony. It must be remembered however, that a sett is a maze of tunnels, often going as deep as thirty feet into the hillside, so it is understandable that the paths of the two probably do not cross very often. This sharing of homes is very rare during the summer, one reason being that rabbits prefer to live above ground during this season, another that the badgers have their young ones and tend to be less hospitable.

THE RABBIT

From early spring until late summer you will, without too much effort, see young rabbits at all stages of growth, for this is when their main breeding takes place. Rabbits are capable of re-mating successfully twelve hours after the birth of a litter, but though this machine-like system is worked on many commercial rabbit farms, in the wild it rarely takes place unless weather conditions are favourable and food is plentiful.

Gregarious by nature, rabbits live together in colonies of varying sizes, but however large or small all are jealously guarded by the most dominant buck which is known as the *King*. This buck's claim to power arises simply from his ability to defeat all contenders to the throne and this power is shared by the *Queen Doe*, a middle-aged matron of great breeding capacity and experience. As royalty, she is the only one allowed to breed within the confines of the main warren, all the other does must leave and dig out the short breeding stops which I have mentioned before. Should they for some reason not do this, their young ones would be killed by the buck, who spends the time he is not preening the Queen patrolling his kingdom, making sure that trespassers are kept out. Generally there is no trouble within the warren, for the other rabbits know their place and respect his position. All the rabbits which are tolerated by the *Queen* are allowed to remain but those who are not, and this usually applies to young bucks, are forcibly ejected with a ferociousness not usually associated with this placid breed. When attacked by other animals rabbits will fight in much the same way as a dog rather than accept death meekly. While incidents like this often occur, as rabbiting men with scarred fingers can testify, in most cases, when attacked, rabbits will neither run away nor make any attempt to defend themselves. Instead they flatten themselves into the ground, close their eyes and scream piteously, waiting for the death blow.

Sometimes their fear is so great that they become virtually paralysed and die before any blow or bite has been given, especially in the case of attack by stoat or weasel.

An interesting point found with both rabbits and hares, is their ability to reabsorb unborn litters back into the tissues of their bodies. This usually takes place when any form of stress is placed upon the pregnant doe, for example, crowded living conditions. What happens is that the development of the young ones is halted within the female at any stage of growth and they dissolve. This has nothing to do with litters that might die from such things as external injuries, for in this case they would be stillborn.

Fortunately, or unfortunately, depending upon whether you are economically affected by them or not, rabbits have still not recovered from the mortal blow they received twenty-one years ago in the form of myxomatosis. This foul disease was first discovered in Britain on an estate near Edenbridge, Kent, during the late summer of 1953. Already known on the Continent, for it was first discovered by an Italian scientist as early as 1896, it was rumoured then, and has never been proved or disproved, that its emergence in this country was brought about deliberately by men importing infected rabbits. Within a short time outbreaks were confirmed in neighbouring Sussex and thereafter it proceeded to travel throughout the country at the rate of roughly ten miles a month. In its wake were left thousands upon thousands of blind, deaf and dying rabbits, in fact ninety per cent of the rabbit population were wiped out.

Fleas transmit this virus disease from animal to animal, but many farmers, impatient for the myxoma virus to reach their land and clear it of a great pest, were reported to be paying substantial sums for live infected rabbits to release onto their property, a practice which is now illegal.

We have further outbreaks every now and again, and even today as the rabbit population grows you might still come across pockets of diseased rabbits though nothing like in the same proportions as in 1953/4.

Hares, which very likely helped to spread the virus by way of fleas, were not susceptible to it themselves, though I must contradict myself straight away by saying that a tiny percentage were found to have contracted the disease, but so small was this that I think the former statement can hold true for the majority.

THE HARE

This is an animal you are most likely to see galloping into the horizon, for when it is stationary it is very difficult to see at all. Many people imagine that there is very little difference between the hare and the rabbit, assuming that because there is a superficial resemblance, they are almost as one. Nothing could be further from the truth, for the habits and existence of the hare are very remote from that of the rabbit. We have two species of hare in Great Britain – the most common being the brown hare, for as its name suggests, the mountain or blue hare is confined to the high districts of the north. Differences however are slight, the three most obvious being that the mountain hare is slightly smaller, has shorter ears, and during the winter months has the protective ability of turning white so as not to be conspicuous amongst the snowy wastes. It is when this white fur is growing out during the spring that they have a bluish appearance – hence the name.

Unlike the gregarious rabbit, the hare is a solitary creature, preferring to live not in underground burrows, but in what are known as *forms* which are simply impressions in long grass. Within these scanty forms the hare trusts to its fur colouring to blend into the background and its own ability to remain frozen to escape detection by passers-by. Its fur is a beautiful tawny colour not unlike that of a tawny owl. So much so, that when a neighbour knocked on my door with, as he put it, *an orphan for you,* at first glance I took the tiny bundle in his hand to be that of a young owl.

One must always beware of orphans or supposedly abandoned creatures, for eight times out of ten this is not the case, particularly with hares. Leverets, as the young are known, are born above ground in a very advanced state, having a good covering of fur, eyes open, and the ability to run around should the need arise. The complete litter, usually numbering three or four, is brought forth in the same form, but after a day or two the female moves them individually to separate forms, and by this action she spreads the obvious risk of losing her whole family to the marauding jaws of fox or badger. During the four weeks until these

Hares *can often outpace enemies by reaching speeds up to sixty miles an hour.*

young ones are weaned, the mother is very rarely out of earshot, ready at all times to come bounding and hissing to their aid should danger threaten. So if you should find a leveret on its own, huddled in the grass, leave it alone.

The chap who brought the leveret to my doorstep was a countryman who knew when and when not to pick up helpless youngsters, but this young hare, while by no means abandoned, had been inadvertently sprayed with an insecticide field dressing. As it was only a week old he presumed, rightly or wrongly, that the parent would find it impossible to trace her offspring due to it being de-scented apart from the fact that the spray may possibly have been harmful to the infant.

As young as it was the leveret hissed defiance at me, though it soon settled down to accept four meals a day of lactol and glucose from a syringe. After a few days it was confident enough to start demanding food, and this it did in the same manner as it would have done in the wild, by drumming its forefeet rapidly and loudly.

For many years zoologists thought that hares slept with their eyes open, for nobody had managed to see them closed. I believe this has now been disproved, but not once during the eight weeks I looked after the baby hare did I see it close its eyes and I tried every ruse I could think of.

When breaking up their scent trail, adults are capable of taking great leaps, often in excess of seventeen feet and as I observed the baby, when no bigger than a cup, making high jumps of thirty inches, this I can well believe. Apart from this prodigious feat, hares have a top speed of sixty miles an hour and are able to turn at right angles to their path without slackening speed, which means that they can outrun most of their enemies, and even give the greyhounds, used for hunting them, a good run for their money.

Being purely vegetarian in diet, the hare is a pest to farmers, market gardeners and particularly foresters. In areas where forestry is an industry, they can wreak havoc among newly planted trees by working their way up and down the lines nipping off the juicy leading shoots. As the normal three foot rabbit fence is no deterrent, the forester has to rely on dog and gun until the young trees have grown tall enough to be out of reach.

By this time a thicket is forming and as hares do not like an enclosed environment, they move out to more open countryside. Apart from this expensive diet, they subsist less harmfully on clover, sweet grass, chicory and thistle.

I mentioned that hares hiss loudly when annoyed and this is only one of the many noises they make, for unlike rabbits they are very vocal. A low grunting tone, with various inflections, denotes different emotions. Teeth grinding is a warning signal and when fighting they grunt and moan loudly enough to draw your attention to the much described spectacle of the *mad March hares* which is simply the male's way of showing off to the females at the onset of the breeding season. Count yourself very fortunate if you do witness these displays during March, for sightings are not as common as the text books would have us believe. I must confess only to have seen this on one occasion.

ANIMAL PLAY

As spring is the time for birth, summer is the time for growing up, gaining strength in the warm days and, for most youngsters, play before taking on the rigours of adulthood. Most young creatures play to varying degrees, for this is the way they practise and learn how to be adults. Carnivorous animals like fox, badger and weasel, frequently play at stalking some symbolic victim – a piece of wood, a scrap of fur, or an old bone. Earlier I mentioned that bluebells and wild garlic were flattened over a great area within the woods near my cottage. The reason for this was that within this area was a fox's earth and the cubs from this earth spent hour after hour boisterously playing king of the castle, hide and seek and many other games up and down these slopes. Evidence such as this often helps to point out where cubs may be watched.

Carnivorous animals tend to play more and for longer than those animals which are generally hunted by them. Young rabbits seem to play at running and jumping games, designed unknowingly to sharpen their escape drill. Hares apart from being solitary, seem quite unlike the rabbits, inasmuch as they are tiny adults as soon as they are born, thus appearing to lack the need to play. The play of tiny squirrels, too, is a preview of their adulthood, for hide and seek amongst the branches with brothers and sisters seems to score high on their list of games.

Otters of all ages seem to enjoy sliding down mudbanks and this I think is play, pure and simple, with no other meaning than that it is great fun. Moreover the leapfrog games of badgers would seem to be in the same category, for age seems no barrier.

It is often mooted that foxes are silent for the majority of the year, only becoming vocal during the January mating season, but I have found that during late July and early August the vixens are surprisingly noisy. This I put down to the cubs who at this time are getting quite big and full of exuberance, often much to the annoyance of their mother, forcing her to quell their high spirits by screaming at them. Badger cubs, while equally as fun-loving never seem to become quite so boisterous.

A FEW SUMMER INSECTS

Right through summer there are so many insects about that it is quite impossible to keep pace with them.

Butterflies are everywhere flitting from flower to flower, for although every species has its own favourite food plant (as do moths) they still visit other types of flowers. However it is only on their special plant that they lay their eggs. If you wish to attract butterflies to your garden invest in the easily grown shrub *buddleia* or, as it is often called, *butterfly bush.* It deserves the name, for in midsummer when its lilac shaped flowers are in full bloom and giving out their glorious scent, they become a mecca for tortoishells, red admirals and many of the peacocks. This plant seems to have a narcotic effect on them, for if you stand near the bush they will settle on your outstretched arms and make no effort to leave, which is certainly not normal behaviour.

The insect which suffers the highest mortality rate at the hand of man, apart from flies, must surely be the wasp. No sooner does its black and yellow body appear within swotting distance than it is hastily crushed amidst a great commotion of armwaving, jumping up and down and panic stricken squeals. I am as guilty of this as anyone, although I try not to be because it is only in late summer that the wasp is a pest. During the rest of the year it kills thousands of harmful insects. It is when the colonies break up and they need to find fresh sources of food that they turn to fruits and foods containing sugar. Every queen wasp killed in April means thousands of offspring less in the late summer, and naturally more fruit (and less stings) but it also means many more insects which cause even more damage. So before you kill a wasp give some thought to its good points which are almost equal to those of the bee which, through education, the average person would not dream of killing. Sadly, the wasp has not been educated, for it is the bee's most dangerous enemy.

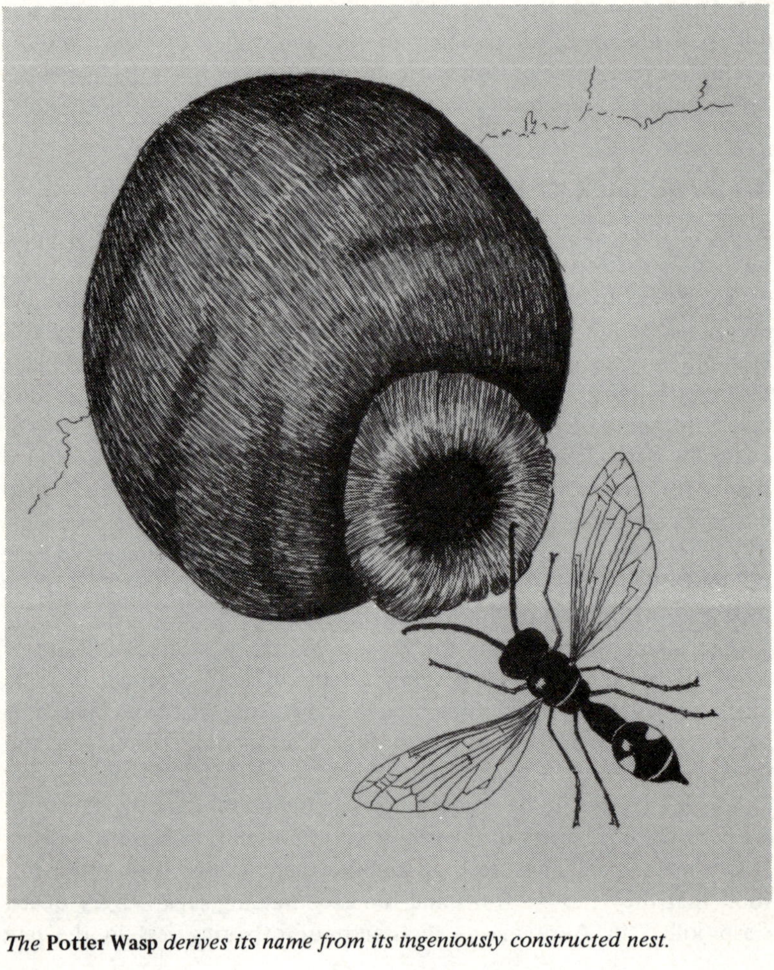

The **Potter Wasp** *derives its name from its ingeniously constructed nest.*

CRICKETS AND GRASSHOPPERS

As I write, the night air outside my window is filled with the sound of crickets and grasshoppers – melodious, rasping chorus that is as reminiscent of summer as the song of the lark or the twittering of swallows. In the wooded glades, in open meadowland, or heather covered moors, the sound of them rises, but have you ever stopped to wonder how this sound is produced? The song is not produced from vocal chords, but in the case of short horned grasshoppers is caused by rubbing a thick vein on the front wing, along the roughened inside edge of the large hind leg. Long horned grasshoppers and related crickets get the same effect by rubbing their forewings together.

Ranging in size from half an inch to two and a half inches, we have twenty-nine species in Britain, but some of these are quite rare, or at least so difficult to see, that it amounts to the same thing. Some of the females have what appears to be a fearsome sickle-shaped sting, but this is simply the organ for egg laying, and perfectly harmless. The reason for its knife-like appearance is because it is used for inserting the eggs, often numbering up to a thousand, into plant stems or the ground.

The famous *Cricket on the Hearth* hardly merits the name in these enlightened days of hygiene, for being an insect that loves debris and refuse abundant in houses of yesteryear, it has been swept out of man's dwellings onto his rubbish dumps, so that is where you must search it out.

Nearly all of the species conform to the accepted appearance, being green or brown and having greatly enlarged hind legs, though overall they vary considerably in size. Yet the strangest and most spectacular is the one most rarely seen – the mole cricket, as its name suggests, spends most of its life underground. An interesting feature of the mole cricket, apart from its appearance, is that when it lies near the surface it builds the entrance of its hole to form a loudspeaker. The entrance is actually two holes, which join up a short distance underground and they are shaped so that the call of the cricket concentrates into a beam. Sitting at the junction of the two holes the cricket rubs its wings together and the resultant sound is amplified up the two tunnels. Directly behind it, in the roof of the burrow, it scrapes out a depression and this prevents the song from going down the hole, instead of out of it to the ears of nearby females as intended.

Generally, the common green grasshopper is the most easily found, but it is worth making a little effort to discover as many others as you can – you never know, you might be fortunate enough to come across the mole cricket, which would put you in a position rarely achieved by the average naturalist.

ANTS

At this time too, watch out for the nuptial flights of the ants, for though they are always with us – much to our annoyance when they invade our larders – this is the time when they are most obvious. It is always the winged males that appear first, closely followed by the females. For some time they swarm on the ground in a seething black mass, then they take flight, as their courtship must always take place in the air. As much as a hundred feet in the air they fly providing a great feast for birds who collect in flocks to pick them out of the sky. After mating, the males drop to the ground and die, but the females come down stronger than ever, shake off their wings, which are no longer needed, and retire underground to begin egg laying. On many occasions I have found this taking place around the hours of ten in the morning and four in the afternoon when the weather is warm.

GLOW WORMS

If you are out in the late evening you may see the pale yellow-green pinpoints of light which are given out by the glow worm. Not a worm but a beetle, both the male and female can produce this light without heat and even the larvae give out a soft glow. These larvae may often be found under the roots of dock leaves and the best time to search them out is after dark with the aid of faint torchlight.

SUMMER'S END

Summer's end, and I have only scraped the surface of the thousands of interesting things which may be seen throughout the countryside during this season. Yet I have always found that if you go out with the intention of seeking one particular item, invariably in the process you stumble across a dozen other things which provoke your interest. Proof of this I found whilst making an intensive study of the fox. It was not enough single-mindedly to follow the habits of this fascinating animal, for time and time again I found myself sidetracked down many avenues, the study of fleas, the comparison of teeth structures amongst various carnivores, how seasons affect day to day life, etc, so that in the end I found myself studying the fox through the vast spectrum of nature in general. For no individual animal, bird or plant is an island, each being in some way dependent on another, interlocking in the jig-saw puzzle of the countryside.

For this reason one cannot get rid of a single species without upsetting the ecological balance of nature or without leaving a gap in the whole, a fact proved when man tried to kill off the rabbit and almost caused an unhealthy imbalance. For what do the predators who feed on rabbits turn to when their traditional supply is cut off. Hares? Lambs? Poultry? Cats? Once begun, where does this meddling with nature end? Because almost all our fauna is a pest to one man or another depending on his livelihood. The squirrel to the forester, the badger to the dairy farmer, the bullfinch to the fruitgrower, and so on. It would be a terrible day when man decided that he could not *afford* the luxury of wildlife.

1. Cranefly : 2. White Admiral : 3. Common Grasshopper : 4. Male Stag Beetle
5. Water Stick Insect : 6. Water Spider : 7. Great Silver Water Beetle

AUTUMN

According to our calendar, autumn is a season that *happens* more or less when it is supposed to. The other seasons seem to drift from one into another and you can hardly mark their beginnings. Normally, the first day of September is still warm and summery, but by the tenth which is the official first day of autumn, cold nights and misty mornings are commonplace. This is no criticism however, for what else can match the crisp splendour of such mornings, when through a hazy mist the earth is bathed in gold and every spider's web is hung with scintillating lights – a beautiful legacy of the night's frost.

For the farmer, the annual harvest is either well on its way or just beginning, depending upon which part of the country it is. Hay will have been cut early in August, for this is a job most farmers like to get out of the way before tackling the harvesting of their specialist crop, whether corn, fruit, hops or vegetables.

For the fruit grower this is a very busy period – he has his crop of apples and pears to attend to, while in many districts plums are still on the trees.

At this time of the year the hedges and spinneys yield up a succulent harvest for any rambler who cares to pause for a while. Blackberries are at their best, for surely this is the most prodigal of all our wild fruits, though generally more prolific in a southern aspect. Raspberries seem to be their opposite number in northern areas. For those who live near moorland or mountainous districts the delicious fruits of the bilberry may be sampled, though some of you may know this low growing plant by more localised names, such as whinberry, whortleberry or worts. Three other edible berries found in similar places are the cowberry, which is often known as the red whortleberry, though it differs from its relation by having pink flowers instead of green, also by having evergreen leaves. Cranberries are another, famous for the sauce made from them to accompany turkey or venison, though I must admit the latter rarely graces my table. Thirdly, there is the cloudberry, a close relation of the blackberry, low growing and having hard yellow fruits not unlike those of the raspberry. All three fruits, however, are not to be recommended straight from the plant as they are bitter to the taste. Nevertheless they are delicious when made into sauces, jellies and jams.

The wild strawberry may be found all over the country in such places as open woods, hedgerows and scrubland. Smaller, but by far sweeter than our cultivated varieties, it is well worth searching out. Sloes, as the fruits of the blackthorn are known, are by appearance deceptively mouth-watering, for while looking like small plums, their skins have the colour and bloomed texture of expensive black grapes. They are intensively bitter, but make very tasty jelly and wine. In the distilling trade they are used for adding extra piquant flavour to gin.

SEEDS

A simple fact that may easily be overlooked in the enthusiasm of filling mouths and baskets with the seemingly limitless fruits, is that all fruits are simply ripe seed-boxes. And they take many other forms than those one normally expects from the term. Yet whatever their appearance, they all serve the same function – that of protecting the seed or seeds contained within the seed-box, also of scattering them. For seeds must be scattered away from the parent plant otherwise the young seedlings would be cut off from the sunlight or die through overcrowding. So for this reason most plants have some arrangement for the spreading of their seeds and in many cases some are successful in *bribing* humans, birds and animals alike to do this work for them.

Seeds are unaffected by passing through the digestive systems of animals or humans and I would think that many of the harder types actually benefit from such an experience by being softened in the process. Of course many seeds are crushed and digested, and in the same way many nut-fruits are eaten by squirrels and others, yet many more are hoarded in the ground and never retrieved. So while these

Grey Squirrel

Dandelion

animals destroy many seeds they do more than just spread the remainder, they actually plant them.

Even children playing with conkers or sycamore *spinners* are helping, for while some are damaged and broken, many more are thrown here and there eventually to root.

Some fruits, not attractive enough to rely on being eaten, take the matter into their own hands and spread their seeds by physical force, sometimes violently, sometimes more gently.

Examples of the violent approach may be observed in such plants as broom, gorse, herb robert – which is a relative of the garden geranium – wood sorrel and those four varieties of balsam. The evocative names of two of the varieties of balsam bear witness to their explosive characteristics – jumping jack and touch-me-not; the latter two are known as orange and small balsam respectively. The slightest touch will send the seeds of these plants bursting out like stones from a catapult leaving the fruit, which is the dry pod, still clinging to the bush. Collectively these are known as *dry box fruits.*

The less dramatic method is illustrated by fruits such as poppies and pimpernels. When the petals have withered and fallen, tiny holes open up just below the flat top of the cup shaped poppy-head. When the breeze blows and shakes the poppy head, seeds are sprinkled out like pepper from a pepper-pot. The seed boxes of the pimpernels, bog, yellow and scarlet, are hard round balls. When ripe they part around the middle and the upper half falls off leaving the seeds to be sprinkled out by the breeze.

Of those seeds spread by the wind, the best known are thistledown and dandelion. Who has never tried to tell the time by blowing on dandelion *clocks*? Each of the little parachutists that drift away on the breeze are whole fruits, or nutlets containing a single seed. Similarly, fruit and seed are practically the same thing in the wild clematis or traveller's joy – the whole fruit has a long feathery parachute attached to its tip. Before the wind has detached the clematis fruits from the plant, you will understand why one of its popular names is *old man's beard.*

The prolific willow herbs also spread their seeds on silky down. The seed pod, or fruit, has four flaps which open from the top releasing the seeds on cottony wings. I say prolific, because this plant seems to spring up everywhere – building sites, quarries, railway embankments, rubbish dumps – in fact wherever there is ugliness they seem to be at their best. In summer their deep-pink or mauve flowers add colour and beauty where there would otherwise be none. For this reason it is known in Canada as *fire-weed* as it is always the first plant to cover up the blackened wastes caused in areas devastated by forest fire.

Many seeds have wings, rather than parachutes – generally those from trees such as pine, birch, maple, elm and willow. In the case of the pine, the fruit, which is the familiar cone, ripens and the scales gape open releasing the winged seeds. The fruits and seeds of the birch, maple, elm and willow are combined and both fall in a gentle spinning motion when broken loose by the breeze.

Finally, we have the method of *attachment* as a means of spreading seeds. As mentioned in the summer section, many grasses use this method, but the two most common plants which disperse their seeds in this manner are burdock and cleavers. The former has a fruiting-head, or burr, which is really a tight cluster of fruits each having a stiff sharp hook. These become hooked onto the wool or fur of animals and could be carried many miles before the host paused to comb them off. In Scotland I always recognised the plant cleavers by the name of *sticky willy* and certainly no name could be more well deserved, for not only the tiny green fruits are covered by many hooklets, but also the leaves and the trailing stems. This plant is also known as *goosegrass* because long ago it was used to feed newly hatched goslings.

Before I leave the subject of fruits, I would like to stress as strongly as possible that children should never eat wild fruits without the supervision of an adult. If children get into the habit of eating edible fruits unsupervised, there is always the risk that they might one day sample the visually attractive fruits of our nine poisonous berries. It is not enough to tell them only to eat blackberries, for a child might easily confuse these with the fruits of the belladonna, or deadly nightshade, Britain's most poisonous berries. Three of these are sufficient to cause death to a child. Describing each poisonous berry is not enough; do this by all means, but stress the fact that no wild fruits should be eaten unless an adult says that they are safe.

Strangely enough, berries which are poisonous to humans have no effect whatsoever on the many birds that feed on them. Which rather undermines the advice sometimes given to those who might have had to live off the land in some inhospitable jungle – *if it doesn't kill animals, it won't kill you.*

AUTUMN LEAVES

Though early autumn is the harvest time of the year, it is really trees which come to mind when this season is mentioned. Only when the leaves begin to change their colours from many shades of green to copper brown and gold are we are convinced that autumn is with us and summer has faded.

Just when this colour change takes place varies enormously. Some years, autumn, in this sense, arrives in September; other years it does not arrive until October or even November. The American expression *the Fall* is a most descriptive phrase for this time of the year. The fall of the leaves happens so regularly we tend to take it for granted, without ever wondering why this phenomenon takes place.

The alteration which takes place in each leaf is not so much a sign of decay, but rather the symptom of a new vigorous process. All summer the leaves have been carrying out a vital task of catching and *bottling* the sunlight. They have been manufacturing a valuable fluid, and this precious liquid is not to be wasted. So when the lower suns of autumn check the leaves' vitality, this fluid begins to flow back into the twigs and branches of the tree. This explains why you will see leaves which have lost their greenness around the edges, yet still retain a green band along the central veins. When this ebbs, the leaves of all deciduous trees have played their part and, their function completed, they fall to the ground. This removal of the leaves without some form of protection would result in an open wound being left in the tree through which sap would *bleed* and disease would gain entry. To prevent this, the tree gradually rejects the leaf by growing a layer of cork-like cells across the base of the stalk. This layer is known as the *abscission layer* and its existence perfectly caulks and bandages the broken spot. By cutting a section through both leaf and the twig to which it is attached, this layer may be seen clearly under the lens of a magnifying glass. Incidentally, it is by means of the resultant scars that we can often identify the barest of twigs in winter as the scar on each species of tree or shrub is differently arranged and consistent for each species in question. The most familiar example of these distinctive markings are those of the horse chestnut – the scar being similar in design to a horseshoe, even to the nail marks.

Though often overlooked a similar happening takes place with twigs as well as leaves. Small, lifeless branches fall from many trees, particularly willows, to a degree which is comparable to the autumnal shedding of leaves. This is not the result of decay, but is an effort on the part of the tree to rid itself of superfluous twigs and the process is again deliberate rejection.

The blaze of autumnal colour, resulting from the gradual leaf rejection is beautiful compensation for the loss of the greens. All shades of brilliant colours leap to the eye – the coppery tints of the beeches, the pale yellow of elms, the deeper gold of the larches, the dull brown and burnt ochre of English oaks, the cherry, pear, thorn and spindle streaked with orange, red and purple, and the marvellous red-yellow flame brilliance of the English maple. While here and there are patches of deep colour added by such fruits as the deep purple haws, the gleaming orange of rose hips and the sparkling reds of guelder rose, spindle and black and white bryony.

Of course, not all the leaves of our trees fall at the same time, which is obvious if we take a look through a mixed wood. For we find some of the trees still green, others diffused with variegated colours and others quite bare already. It is an interesting fact that many of those trees which are late in breaking into leaf are very often among the first to lose their leaves, in many cases while they are still green. Ash and lime trees may in this respect be likened to the swift. In the avian world the swift is very often the last to arrive in this country but invariably the first away.

GALLS

Some galls are familiar to everyone, for example the oak apple, others are not quite so well known. But in most cases these obviously abnormal forms of growth create a puzzle for beginners in the study of botany, for there is no external sign to betray their origin. Primarily the creation of these galls are the workings of animal organisms, such as gall flies, gall wasps, eel worms, mites, a few beetles and some moth caterpillars, while sometimes bacteria is the culprit. The incipient cause is brought about by any one of these insects laying their eggs in parts of the tree or plant. Any part may be so attacked, from the youngest shoot to the deepest root in the soil, and wherever eggs or bacteria are present a gall results, varying from the minute dots which appear in some leaves, to the sometimes gigantic *witches' brooms* which may be seen on such trees as birch, hornbeam and willow, as vast twiggy outgrowths.

It used to be thought that the affected tree or plant was responsible for these strange growths, the idea being that it was some form of protection by the plant to prevent the insects from burrowing deeper into the tissue. This idea was soon refuted when it was discovered that when the eggs are laid, an acid is introduced at the same time which changes the growth formation of the host. With some of the gall-making species, nothing happens until the eggs hatch, then as soon as this takes place the larva themselves produce acid and gall begins to form. Once the gall is formed, the larva surrounded by a thickening wall of tissue, feeds on the cells contained within.

Usually each gall is peculiar to one species of plant or tree and will not be found on any other. However, the oak and some other trees have more than one type of parasite upon them. The most well-known is the marble gall, and as the name suggests is round and roughly the size of a marble. Often this type is wrongly called the oak apple, but if you carefully cut open a green, unripe marble gall, you will discover one single larva nestling in the centre. Whereas if you were to cut open a true oak apple, which is soft in texture and irregularly shaped, you would find not one, but six to eight tiny larvae. Both these galls are caused by separate species of gall-wasps. You may also find on the leaves or on the long flower-stalks of the oak, the currant gall which resembles red currants, both in size and appearance. The eggs of the insect responsible for these are laid in the buds, but the actual galls do not appear until long after the oak-catkin has grown. An interesting point is that while unaffected catkins drop off once flowering is over, those that bear galls remain on the tree. This is an indication that the tree has lost control over these parts and is unable to reject them, as it can with those catkins which are unaffected. Other common oak galls are those known as spangle, of which there are a number, each being made by one stage of a distinct species of insect. They are to be found clustered on the underneath side of leaves and it can prove interesting to collect the various types to find out what emerges. Then there are the cherry galls, similar in appearance to marble galls, but growing from the leaves as opposed to the buds. Artichoke galls are not unlike the flowering head of hop plants, though slightly smaller. These grow from the tip of young oak shoots. It would be possible to find all these galls mentioned and a few others growing on one tree at the same time and it is not unusual to find three or four species on one twig.

On the wild rose you will find what is probably our finest gall, the bedeguar gall, more often known as *robins' pin cushion.* This beautifully mossy outgrowth consists of a bright red mass of tough, wiry fibres which make even the straggliest rose bush look conspicuous, as the galls flame out from the angle of the shoots. These growths are at their best in early autumn, though the tiny grubs snuggled inside will not chew their way out of their individual cells until spring arrives. All galls, or I should say, tenants of galls, are parasites. Yet by some poetic justice many of them are in turn preyed upon by other insects. Some of the intruding species wait until a gall is fully formed before killing off the rightful owners and laying their own eggs. Others are true parasites, commonly from a group known as *chakid*. These do not kill the original larva but instead they lay their eggs upon them which, after a time, hatch and feed on the host, much in the same way as fleas do on dogs, or ticks on sheep. Very often the species that ousted the originallarva and took over the home-gall themselves become hosts to invading chakids.

Also on the rose you might discover the bright green rose pea galls growing on the underside of the leaf; and on the leaves of the willow you will see the raised black blisters caused by the sawfly, projecting on both the upper and the lower sides of the leaves. This type is so common that hardly any willow escapes it and many people have the impression that these galls are a normal part of the tree's growth.

There are many other types of galls produced by other insects. They attack not only trees, but cereal crops, vegetables and other valuable plants. See how many you can collect and identify in a season. I have not tried to name insects that cause specific galls, for in most cases the individuals do not have *popular* names, their Latin nomenclature being the only reference. At the same time, while many insects cause completely different galls, they may still only belong to one order such as the gall wasp group, or the saw fly group.

Such is the complexity of trees, their growth, their general constitution and the host of life which teems among their branches or burrows under their *skin*, that one could fill a large volume on this subject alone. Although I said earlier that autumn belongs to the trees, at the same time it is one of the most important seasons so far as wild creatures are concerned.

As a matter of convenience, we begin each new year on the first day of January, an arbitrary date, selected by early man when designing the calendar, as our only means of knowing the exact beginning of any month or any season. Wild creatures have no such written indication. They are governed by food availability, the state of the weather and current temperatures. Their year, like the farmer's year, begins in autumn. To us, this may seem a strange time to begin anything, for surely spring would be much better, but when you give the matter some thought it does not seem so odd. Animals, birds and the majority of insects have at last finished the arduous task of rearing families. After a short breather, they will begin preparations to face the tremendous struggle once again. The birds have moulted and those that spend their winters abroad have already left on their long journeys, leaving the remainder to spend a comparatively quiet time with us.

There are only two species of our wildlife which have the autumn beginnings of their year as their mating season. Bats, which we have examined in an earlier section, are one of these species. The other is that of our wild ungulates – deer.

DEER

Though we have a good representative population of wild deer, the best the amateur naturalist can hope for is a fleeting glimpse or a more prolonged view from some distance away. Both shy and elusive, possessing extremely acute perceptory senses, they are very difficult to

Red Deer Stag

observe in the wild. Of course, most wild life parks have at least one group, normally tame and very easy to watch and photograph. So from the point of anatomical study, the opportunities are perfect. But captive animals can give you no real insight into their natural habits, even when their enclosure covers a few acres, nor can the watcher gain the feeling of achievement and excitement which is aroused by the rare sight of creatures carrying out their daily lives, completely unaware that they are under scrutiny.

Of the seven species of deer living wild in Britain only two, the red and the roe, are native, the direct descendants of our original fauna. All the other species have been introduced into our countryside at varying times. The earliest introduction was that of the fallow deer, which was brought here from Asia Minor by the Romans, for the express purpose of adding another specimen for their hunting pleasures. The muntjac and Chinese water deer are introductions of comparatively recent times, for they were placed in parks during 1890 and 1940 respectively. Escapees from these parks soon bred and spread rapidly throughout the south and Home Counties. The sika deer arrived here from Japan in the 17th century and soon formed substantial herds. Finally we have the reindeer, introduced in 1952 to the Cairngorms in Scotland as an experiment by a Lapp farmer, and while we have only a herd of roughly one hundred at present, their growing numbers are heartening. Their appearance in the Highlands is not a completely new one, for they were common in Scotland until the 12th century, when sadly they were hunted to extinction.

William the Conqueror, although a fanatical hunter of the red, roe and fallow deer, was at the same time their greatest champion. He made absolute their protection from the rabble by creating harsh laws against those who might harm them (himself and his followers excluded). He created vast forests where deer, and other creatures destined for the hunt, could roam. This does not mean that he grew, as if by magic, extensive woodlands – for in those days the term *forest* meant land that was without *(lat-foris)* common law. Instead this land was governed by special laws which preserved the monarch's hunting. Therefore, much forestland contained hundreds of acres which had no trees whatsoever. Another term to cover this type of land was *Royal Chase.* Today Epping Forest is all that remains of the royal forest or Waltham, an area that

Fallow Deer. *Rarely found in large herds, preferring to roam in small groups of about half a dozen.*

once covered some sixty thousand acres in south-west Essex. The New Forest in Hampshire is the largest remaining medieval forest.

In these forests no fences could be put up higher than the level at which a doe and her fawn could easily jump. Farmers were not allowed to chase deer from their crops, even though they suffered financial hardship as a result and no one was allowed to erect buildings in case the increased traffic of men and dogs *might frighten the beestes from their food.* Anyone who killed a hart or hind (male and female red deer) whether by accident or intent, would suffer the penalty of being blinded and anyone caught chasing a deer from the Forest, again by accident or intent, would, if he were a freeman, pay a heavy fine. If he were a bondsman (slave) he would be put to death. All dogs in Royal Chase districts had to have three claws on their forefeet cut close to the foot, to prevent them chasing deer, and many dog owners must have gone in fear and trembling, for whatever crimes their dogs committed against deer the owners suffered the punishment. Naturally, with these protections the deer thrived and their herds grew large, thus guaranteeing the continuance of the race.

This is a prime example of how the hunting of an animal can help to protect it. This form of protection still takes place today, though to a lesser degree, through the pursuit of foxes, otters and deer.

All our deer are gregarious creatures, and prefer living together in groups, though the red deer tends most towards this inclination. Red deer could normally be referred to as living in herds and a stag with twenty or more followers is not an uncommon sight. The other species would more likely be seen in small groups of about half a dozen in number.

Like cattle, deer have a complicated digestive system including a four-sectioned stomach, by the aid of which a great amount of green food can be cropped, swallowed, then chewed at leisure. Ruminating or *chewing the cud* as it is commonly called, is a great advantage to animals who have to feed in exposed positions whilst in constant fear of attack. They can gulp down their food, then retire to a more sheltered place to masticate in safety. Now that bear, wolf and lynx are extinct in this country, the deer's only fear need be of man, although occasionally, during a particularly harsh winter, the smaller species might fall foul of hungry foxes.

Deer always have been, and still are, creatures of deep woodland. However, with man's relentless encroachment into woods and forests they are forced to feed in the unnatural habitat of crop fields. By doing so many of them sign their own death warrants, for a small herd can cause damage worth hundreds of pounds in a single night and no farmer will stand aside and allow this to happen.

Dawn and dusk are their feeding times so if you wish to spot them, this is when you must position yourself and I would suggest the best place would be where extensive woodland abutts fields of growing crops.

Berries, ferns and grass are, from an economic point of view, some of the less important items of their diet. The real damage arises when they chew inroads into root crops and cereals. In forestry country their liking for young tree shoots, leaves and bark causes havoc in plantations.

For deer, autumn is the rutting or mating season and it is at this time the males seem to find their voices; during the rest of the year they are comparatively silent apart from occasional warning barks. The purpose of this autumn voice is to attract females and to discourage or challenge other males who might be in the vicinity. Jealously protective of their family groups, all males become quite savage at this time, so it is advisable to give them a wide berth. Even the harmless little roebuck and the smaller muntjac have been known to cause serious injury to man on more than one occasion.

Mating is over by November and the family groups wander peaceably together over their feeding territories until the following May. Then they break up, the females to find seclusion for the birth of their young, and the males to shed their antlers and hide themselves away, while their new antlers are budding. Normally only the males have antlers, but with reindeer, both male and female have fine headsets. In the case of the Chinese water deer, however, neither sex grows antlers; instead, the males of this species have greatly elongated canine teeth which form tusks.

THE PHEASANT

It is while you are stalking through misty woodlands with bated breath and hushed tread that an explosion of whirring wings and a devastating cry of *kok, kok, kok* will make you stop in your tracks, suddenly aware of the pheasant. By the time this bird has made a noisy crash landing in the trees ahead, any deer you might have glimpsed will have melted speedily into the distance. However, why not practise your stalking prowess by getting closer to the cause of your lost sport, for the pheasant can provide an equally rewarding spotting session.

It is the cock pheasant, resplendent in his brilliant uniform, which normally catches the eye. The female is clad in more subdued colours of buffish-brown and the reason for this, as with most ground nesting birds, is so that she will not be noticeable when sitting on her clutch of eggs.

The most common of our various breeds of pheasant is the ring necked pheasant, the name arising from the very conspicuous white ring around the neck. These are direct descendants of pheasants first brought into this country by the Romans around 1060, though the original species did not have the white ring. Since introduction in the eighteenth century, two other breeds have established themselves as self-supporting wild birds, namely the golden pheasant and Lady Amherst's pheasant. The first is likely to be encountered in woodland areas of the south east Midlands, and is exotically coloured. Its head and neck are marked boldly with black and white plumage. The male has a body colour of beautiful dark green and white, whilst the female is generally pale brown. The golden pheasant has ensconced itself in the woods and heathlands of East Anglia, and is easily recognised by its brilliant red plumage, long golden hued crown feathers and an exceptionally long tail. However, I will refer to all breeds as simply *pheasant*, for their habits are identical.

Although thousands of pheasants are artificially reared every year for the purpose of providing sport for guns, we still have a considerable wild population, which, even if they were not protected, would survive completely by their own efforts.

The rearing of pheasants is done on a semi-domesticated scale and this is carried out by placing chicks, which have hatched from incubated eggs, into enclosures which are often as large as an acre or more. Other than protecting the growing chicks from predators and throwing down food, they are left to their own devices. Then when they are able to fly, they make their way over the enclosure fencing to settle in the surrounding country ready for the pheasant shooting season which begins on 1st October. Naturally, many wild pheasants are attracted into the pens or into the area, so swelling the number of *kills* for the guns. This sport is now a major rural industry, for while *laying down* pheasants is an expensive business, the returns from groups of business men willing to pay thousands of pounds for the shooting rights are tremendously lucrative. Equally, the rewards of poaching these expensive birds have always made them a target for the unscrupulous. Nowadays this underworld industry is carried out on a large scale, as is the rustling of sheep and cattle, a crime not exclusive to the wild west. In the days when every village had its old poacher, his methods for capturing pheasants were often as cruel as they were ingenious. Lighting small fires on the windward side of roosting-trees, then throwing on a handful of sulphur, was guaranteed to bring insensible birds tumbling to the ground, overcome by the fumes. Less humane was the method of inserting hogs' bristles into soaked peas. Having eaten these lethal peas, the pheasants were rewarded by the bristles springing open and painfully choking them to death. Similarly raisins were often baited with fish hooks, with even more painful consequences.

During the winter months pheasants invariably roost in trees, high in the branches when the weather is mild, low down when high winds might topple them from their perches. The rest of the year is spent exclusively on the ground and taking advantage of this many a poacher has crept up and thrown a net over as many as fifteen birds huddled close together. To foil such unsporting (and illegal) behaviour, gamekeepers would stick short thorny branches into the ground where their pheasants were prone to roost. This no doubt brought tears of rage to the eyes of poachers, who had spent many painstaking hours knotting their very fine nets by hand, only to have them torn to pieces.

The most likely places frequented by pheasants are thick woods in the neighbourhood of water, where there is plenty of ground cover in the form of tall weeds, bramble and furze bushes, rushes, ferns and long grass. In a similar way to the aforementioned deer, they make forays from these sheltered spots out into the fields, where the cocks are

Cock Pheasant

particularly conspicuous as they strut up and down, occasionally breaking into vociferous honking as they call the hens to their side.

In April or May the female scratches a shallow depression in the ground, usually underneath the cover of a low bush or long grass. As with most ground-nesters, the nest is quite unsophisticated, containing only the merest lining of leaves or grass. Here she lays on an average ten or twelve pale olive coloured eggs, though it would not be rare to find a nest containing as many as twenty-two. Shortly after emerging from the eggs, pheasant chicks are able to run about and forage for their own food and fluffy leggy chicks following the mother hen is one of the more rewarding sights of early summer.

It is said that if pheasants were more numerous they would rank alongside the pigeon as being destructive feeders, for they can consume enormous quantities of grain, peas, beans, carrots and other valuable crops. In their favour is the fact that they consume vast amounts of wireworms, which are a serious pest of root crops and incidentally are the larval stage of the *click beetle*, so-named because when they topple onto their backs, they right themselves by flexing their bodies with a resounding *click*. The pupae of ants, normally erroneously called eggs, are also eaten with relish while, as mentioned in the spring section, froghopper larvae or cuckoo spit insects are consumed with fatal results for young pheasants. In the woods they eat acorns, beech mast and roots of various wild plants.

Unwilling to fly and clumsy on the wing, pheasants are prey to a host of carnivores, foxes, stoats and weasels being their predominant animal enemies. Though for such apparently tame looking exotics cock pheasants can be veritable dervishes when the need arises. With the vicious spur claw they have on their legs they have been known to rout a fox and I heard a well authenticated story of one demon pheasant which killed a large tom-cat.

While the woods are ringing with the sounds of gunshot and the frantic whirring of wings as the pheasant shoots get into their stride, another *sporting* season is just beginning – that of fox cub hunting.

CUBBING

Truthfully this is not what one would call a season in the true hunting sense, but more of a preliminary. Traditionally cub hunting begins when the last of the corn is cut, and ends officially with the opening of fox hunting proper in November.

The typically British sport of hunting cubs or adult foxes has taken place for hundreds of years in spite of considerable controversy. I will attempt to explain the reason for these early autumn hunts.

Firstly, you must not imagine that the term *cub hunting* refers to the spectacle of hounds running down tiny, defenceless fluffy-coated cubs. By September, the youngsters born in late March or early April

Though only six months old, this **Fox** *cub is very capable of looking after itself.*

are almost fully grown, fit, strong, sharp of wit and cunning and in fact will only be called cubs until they reach sexual maturity in late December. Also by September they have left the vixen, to fend for themselves and to lead their own lives. At the same time, the new entry of hounds into the pack – which entered the kennels as youngsters from what is known as a *walk* the previous spring – commence hunting. So, in effect, the inexperienced hounds are introduced to inexperienced young foxes.

Each year there are many more foxes born than could be tolerated within a given area, so when out cubbing, the field (hunt master and followers) surrounds coverts where cubs are known to be laying up, and by cracking their whips, halloooing loudly and generally creating a frightful noise, they try to prevent any cubs escaping until some of them have been killed. Mature foxes, wise in the ways of the hunt, always slip away at once and no manner of noise can prevent them, nor is it expected to. Also those cubs who have courage and better physical condition escape. Therefore it is the weakest who are invariably put down. Obviously, if a cub receives this sort of treatment on a number of occasions, its sense of survival will be strengthened and it will become an adversary with more than a sporting chance against the hounds when the season proper gets under way. Incidentally, this ringing of the coverts is the only time when the field is allowed to assist or take part in a hunt in any way. At all other times they must be as their collective name suggests simply *followers*.

While cubs have to learn how to be hunted, young hounds also have to learn their job, which is to hunt foxes, and only foxes – nothing else. They must disregard their natural doggy tendencies to chase after rabbits, to snap up hares, pheasants, partridges and cats and must learn to range away from the heels of the huntsman's horse, where hitherto they had been taught to stay. It is most important that they are educated in the meaning of the various tones and blasts of the horn. They must also learn how to creep, wriggle or sometimes crawl on their bellies through flesh-tearing bramble thickets, to climb wire netting and to go under or over gates. So cubbing is more of an in-kennel exercise in character forming and discipline for the hounds, a period in which they quickly learn their craft and find a love for the chase. Many learned hunters express the opinion that foxes find equal pleasure in *the heat of*

A six week old **Fox** *cub.*

the chase, but as this can only be answered subjectively, I will leave you to make up your own minds. I know what I think.

SOME RIVER LIFE – THE PIKE

Whilst eager sportsmen are aiming guns to the sky or tearing hell for leather across undulating countryside behind packs of hounds, another section of this fraternity are baiting their hooks for that veritable wolf of the river – the pike. For 1st October heralds yet another *season* in which the pike is the principal quarry. To observe and study any of our fish, you must be an angler, for fish are rarely accommodating enough to pose for any length of time in crystal clear pools. However, if you do not number angling as one of your pursuits, a glimpse is better than nothing.

Pike favour ambush as a method of attack and they lie in close to the

A **Pike** *will kill and eat anything it is capable of overpowering.*

reeds or other vegetation trusting in their greenish-brown colouration to blend them into the background. From here with a thrust of their powerful tail they shoot out and grasp any fish which happens to be near. So these are the areas in which you must look out for this, our largest and fiercest predator of freshwater, rivers and lakes.

During early spring pike spawn in shallow, heavily weeded water, shedding their numerous eggs liberally over the vegetation. For their first year after hatching from the eggs the young pike, known as *jacks*, remain hidden in the shallows practising their predacious feeding habits, which will make them the scourge of the waters when they grow bigger and subsequently attack larger prey. In these early days jacks will eat virtually anything that moves and is small enough for them to tackle. Insect larvae, tadpoles, small fry or other fish, efts (young newts) and even water snails and beetles are gobbled up. As they grow, pike gradually move out into deeper waters and, while still eating all manner of small titbits, are now capable of snapping up frogs, newts, water voles and medium sized fish of any species. Naturally the larger the pike, the larger its victim, and moorhens, ducks – and on one occasion I heard of even an otter cub – all go to help curb their insatiable appetite. Once grasped in the pike's gaping jaws, escape is virtually impossible, for the lower jaw is ringed with upright needle-sharp teeth which are used for seizing prey, while the complete roof of the mouth bristles like a hairbrush with tiny backward-facing teeth which make withdrawal impossible. It has been estimated that a five-pound pike will consume some fifty pounds of fish annually, so if pike of greater weights have a comparative food intake, their destruction of valuable fish such as trout or salmon must be colossal. For this reason they cannot be tolerated in waters where other fish are being bred.

EELS

At this time of the year pike must make gluttons of themselves on the hundreds of eels migrating to their birthplace – the sea – for the purpose of breeding. In this period eels may be found in all kinds of unexpected places – in small streams, water filled ditches, drain culverts and often overland, where they are mistaken for snakes, wriggling along through the grass. This is made possible by breathing aerated water which they carry in their gills. The distances between waters are not very great and this strange behaviour only takes place during or shortly after rainfall, which often led country folk to believe that it had been raining eels!

Eels are common in most waters of Britain, for where the fashionably modern disease of pollution has killed or driven away other species of fish, they still seem able to thrive. Although they are so familiar in our waters, not one of them was born here. Their spawning grounds are in the depths of the Atlantic, some three thousand miles from the British coastline. Once hatched, the elvers, as the young are known, begin an immense journey which takes three years. Flat, leaf-like, and transparent, they swim with a leisurely, swaying motion, allowing themselves to be carried along by coastal currents. It is not until they reach our coasts that they become the active wriggling creatures so familiar in the spring journeys upstream, which are known as *eel-fare*. Their immigration always takes place in daylight and should the sun disappear behind a cloud, the elvers hide under the banks and water plants. When the sun shines again they continue on their way. In contrast the *eel-run*, or return journey of mature eels, takes place at night.

This autumn return to the sea takes place after the fish have spent several years feeding and growing in freshwater. Their food during this time is as varied as that of the pike and consists of crayfish, worms, frogs, fish, insects and any rodents that are unwary enough to swim in eel-infested waters. Once maturity is reached, the race for the sea begins and no obstacle is insurmountable – hence their passage across land and along ditches as they skirt lock gates and dams. In the estuaries they gradually become acclimatised to the salt water, they then enter the sea and head westwards considerably faster than the speed at which they had travelled as elvers. There will be no third journey for these eels, as once they have deposited their spawn in the darkness of the three-mile-deep Atlantic, they die. However the eel population is kept up by the arrival of new elvers each spring. Try to make a point of seeing their springtime entry, then compare the sizes and conditions of those in the autumn exit.

Even more spectacular than the *eel-run* is the journey of what must be our most handsome fish – the salmon.

THE SALMON

Salmon provide a somewhat parallel case, for like the eel they travel thousands of miles for the purpose of spawning, yet with a difference – their journey is in reverse. Female salmon lay their eggs in British rivers, often as many as fifteen thousand over a short period in shallow holes scooped out of the gravel riverbed. As with most fish, some reptiles and many insects, laying vast numbers of eggs allows for the thousands which will be eaten by predators.

The tiny fish hatched from those eggs which survive are called fry or alevins and at first they lurk amongst the gravel, living on the remains of egg yolk that is still attached to their bodies. At this stage many of them fall prey to the jaws of equally young pike and other predacious creatures. After a month they become more active, moving up and down the river and in turn preying themselves on other small creatures. At one year old, they are rechristened and are now known as *parr*. At this time of their lives they are not dissimilar to trout, for they have spotted markings along their sides which they will wear for four years of growth in freshwater rivers, until these marks are gradually obliterated by a dense silvery coloured pigment, which means they are ready for their emigration to the sea. With their new colour comes a new name, so it is *smolts* that set off for the sea, their inbuilt compasses aimed for the coasts of Europe.

Once in the salt waters they lose their brilliantly silver colouration and become bluish-green, a colour which they retain during the one to four-year stay in foreign waters, a time spent in feeding and growing. Now comes the momentous period of their lives, for large, fit and vigorous, they are ready to travel thousands of miles back to the very same stretch of water in which they were spawned. How they do this is as much a mystery as the way in which swallows, pigeons and cats, to name but a few, can also find their way back to their birthplace with uncanny accuracy. Back in freshwater once more, they change colour to that which one expects from salmon, becoming greenish or brown, mottled with orange or red and marked with dark spots. One more thing – yes, you've guessed it – they are now called *grilse.*

Their aim now is to get as high as possible to the shallows of the tributaries before spawning, and this sight must be one of the most magnificent that nature can give us. Nothing can daunt them, as with fanatical persistence they press on, up our western rivers overcoming obstacle after obstacle in the form of waterfalls, rapids and weirs. Again and again a salmon may leap at a foam flecked waterfall, which might be as high as twelve feet, only to fall back into the pool below. Yet after a brief rest it will try again, until finally it hurls itself over the top of the barrier and continues its journey until brought to a temporary halt by yet another obstacle. It has been found that when salmon leap from the water their speed is between eighteen and twenty miles per hour.

Somewhere in the shallow upper reaches of the river their fantastic journey ends and the breeding cycle has turned full circle as the females deposit their eggs. With spawning over, the adults are weak, flabby and emaciated, and no wonder after their breathtaking efforts. Many of them die in this condition, but those that manage to return to the sea stand a good chance of recovering and making the spawning journey once more. By the way, at this stage they are known as *kelts.*

The **Otter** *is perfectly adapted for a life spent in and around water.*

THE OTTER

Salmon, in a weakened state after spawning, make an easy prey for otters. In fact these aquatic carnivores often follow the fish to their breeding grounds for this very reason. Though designed for a life in water, with their streamlined bodies, webbed feet and waterproof coats, they do not have to rely on their prey being weak, for they are formidable hunters.

In spite of the fact that the otter is not as rare as is commonly believed, it is an extremely difficult animal to see and sightings are usually made by accident rather than intent. One reason for their elusiveness is that they are constantly on the move, seldom spending very long in one district. Even when food is plentiful it seems they cannot alter this nomadic habit, and will travel overland for as much as fifteen miles in a night to reach fresh feeding grounds. If an otter has not reached water by the time the sun comes up, it will bed down in woodland undergrowth or a dry ditch until dusk, when the journey will be resumed.

It might surprise you to learn that the otter is closely related to the tiny but ferocious stoat and also the badger. Yet were you to observe these three, and others within this same family, you would see likenesses in their appearance and habits.

When fully grown, the average length and weight of the otter is in the region of fifty inches (nose to tip of tail), and thirty-five pounds respectively. Between male and female, known as dog and bitch, there is little appreciable difference, apart from the extra weight of the female, normally she is some four or five pounds heavier. However this would not help to determine the sex of an otter without it being seen with the opposite sex for comparison.

Their thick chocolate brown outer-fur is so watertight that the soft undercoat never gets even slightly damp. Also while swimming under water they have the ability of being able to close both ears and nostrils, so added to the fact that they have webbed feet and are beautifully streamlined, you will see how perfectly adapted they have become to a life on and under the water.

On present evidence, it would appear that otters have no definite breeding season, for whelps, as the young cubs are known, have been seen at all months of the year. For many years, naturalists held the opinion that March and April were the peak months for litters, but now facts seem to point towards November and December. Although correct this does seem contrary to normal animal behaviour which commonly favours springtime as the best period in which to produce as this gives the young ones warm weather and a plentiful food supply.

Mating takes place actually in the water and after a gestation period of two months, the bitch produces two, three or occasionally five whelps in the breeding nest or *holt*. This holt is merely a hole in the river bank, a tunnel amongst tree roots overhanging the water, or even disused land drains, rabbit burrows or a fox's earth. At birth the young are blind, but well-covered with a soft grey coloured fur. The waterproof coat, though growing, does not become sufficiently dense until they reach three months of age, when they are ready to enter water for the first time. Like the babies of many semi-aquatic animals, even ducks, the otter cub has a natural aversion of taking the plunge and therefore has to be patiently cajoled into the water. Should this sympathetic treatment not work, the mother will pick up her reluctant offspring and deposit them, mewing and bleating with fear, into the deep end. After a few days no inducement is needed and they are ready to learn the arts of hunting and – more important – the art of survival. Play, often an important part of growing up because games help to sharpen various senses, can be with otters, play – pure and simple. Most mammals treat the rompings of their young with casual indifference, but otter parents join in with equal, if not more, obvious enjoyment. The dog otter only helps to feed the young ones for about six weeks then he leaves, but the bitch continues her life with the cubs long after they have been weaned, only leaving them when she is ready to start breeding again.

There is probably no river in Britain that does not have an otter's holt (breeding nest) or hover (resting nest) somewhere along its length to which an otter will pay a visit at least once in the year. Clues to their presence may be found with diligent searching and once you have found evidence of their pathways of *altars* you will stand a good chance of eventually sighting the creatures who use them, for like the badger, otters use the same routes and *sprainting* areas for decade after decade.

This single-mindedness for favourite pathways often leads to the death of badgers in particular, for if a new motorway cuts across these ancient walks they will continue to follow them, all too often with fatal results.

The *altar*, as already mentioned, is an otter's favourite feeding place or a signpost for those who will follow. Often it is a partially submerged rock, worn smooth by generations of use, not far from the holt or hover. But it could also be a tree stump, the corner of a shingle beach or a well-flattened mud spit. Whatever form it takes, you will find heavy deposits of droppings (known as spraints) which, depending on their age, will tell you whether or not an otter is in the vicinity. When fresh, these droppings are roughly three inches in length, cigar-shaped, and very black and mucoid. After a time, when they dry out, they become light grey in colour, in a similar manner to those of the fox. These droppings may also be found at regular intervals along the otter's boundaries, for even though they do not stay long in one district, while they are there they expect other otters to respect their territorial rights. If dissolved in warm water, these spraints will give you some idea of what the animal has been eating, for they will contain, fish scales, fur, teeth and occasionally feathers.

If you are out at night or early in the morning along the river, you might be fortunate enough to hear the questing call of an otter. Held on a long low note the unmistakable flute-like whistle carried some considerable distance. When alarmed otters hiss and mew like a cat and when frightened or angry will squeal loudly, while blowing grampus-like through the nostrils.

Whether or not you are ever successful in your searches for the otter – and bear in mind that many professional naturalists have never seen one – your wanderings up and down river banks will never have been fruitless. For among the endless variety of interesting forms of nature that you cannot help but notice, it is almost guaranteed that you will see at least one of our other three mammals which have chosen water as their main habitat. One, the water vole, is a native to Britain, the other two, coypu and mink, are species which have been accidentally introduced into the wild, but as they have such a stronghold along our riverways they must be classed as a firm part of our wildlife.

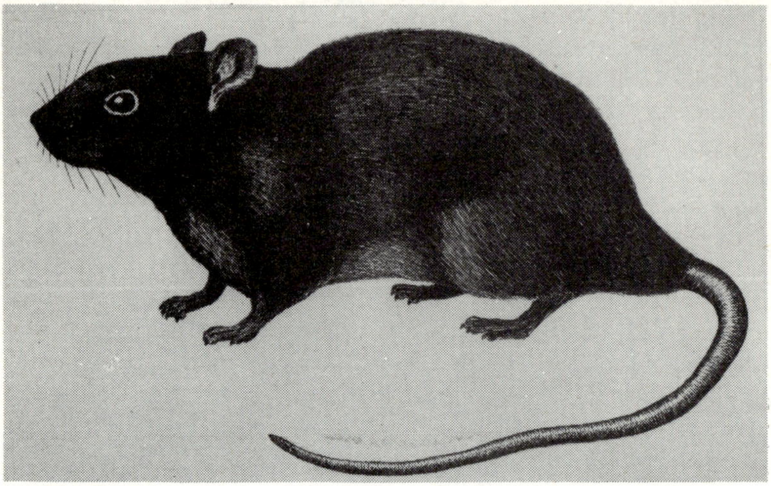

The **Common Brown Rat.**
This species should not be confused with the attractive, inoffensive water vole.

THE WATER VOLE

Before I go into detail about the habits of this charming little rodent, I would like to make it perfectly clear that we have no such animal in Britain as the water-rat, yet one often hears reference to the mythical creature. The common brown rat often takes to water in search of food or to gain access to waterside buildings, but other than this it is strictly a *land-lubber*. On the other hand, the water vole often gains the name of water rat and is killed because of it, yet by nature it is fastidiously clean, characteristically timid and completely harmless. It is also one of the few mammals innocent of any damage to the property of man.

Identification is simple. If you see what you think is a vole swimming on the surface of water, then it is a rat, for voles invariably submerge as soon as they dive in. On the bankside, the difference is that the vole looks more like a smooth-haired guinea pig with a long tail and is roughly the same size. The very blunt face, tiny ears and large round eyes set high on the head help to give it an endearing quality. Incidentally, *Ratty* of *Wind in the Willows* fame, was in fact a water vole.

Found everywhere, even in Ireland where it was thought they did not exist, water voles excavate burrows above the water-line, along streams and rivers with sloping banks plenty of overhanging vegetation and mud banks or sand spits where they may feed and sun themselves in comparative safety. These burrows consist of a rounded chamber near the entrance which is used as a day bed, and further in, another chamber which is the animal's sleeping quarters. Adjoining this bedroom is another chamber used exclusively as a larder for storing food. During autumn the larders are filled to capacity, for while water voles do not hibernate, they tend to spend long periods in their burrows during very cold or inclement weather.

The first clue that water voles are close by you would be the sound of one or two of them diving into the water with a resounding *plop*. Once you have heard this, all you have to do is to look up and down the bankside until you see evidence of plants which have been cleanly bitten off and, possibly, tracks in the mud. Stand quietly for a short time and you will be rewarded by their return and then you can watch them with impunity, for a helpful feature of water voles is that they are terribly short-sighted, so they will not even be able to see you as close as six feet from them. It is amusing to watch them eating greenstuff, which is basically their staple diet, though they will eat fish left by some other predator, but do not kill themselves. The stalks of plants are normally favoured rather than the foliage and the attitude adopted when eating is not unlike that of the beaver. They squat back on their haunches, grip the stalk or root in their forepaws and purposefully feed the length into their mouths. That they are fastidious creatures may be observed by the habit of shaking or brushing off any dirt that adheres not only to the food, but also to their paws before commencing to eat.

Breeding starts in April or May and continues until September, so during the summer months look out for the pretty youngsters emulating their parents or sunning themselves on the bankside. If you have found a burrow earlier in the year, bear in mind that water voles prefer a separate breeding nest away from the normal living quarters. This would not be far away, but could be under a pile of stones, logs, or whatever is convenient. That the females produce from sixteen to twenty young ones during a season is a matter of necessity, as with most small mammals, for their death rate is high. On land they have the usual carnivores to contend with, whilst in the water, herons, pike and large trout all take a heavy toll.

Eight inches in length, the water vole is the largest of our voles. The others – bank vole, short-tailed vole and Orkney vole – are more mouselike in size. But all have the same vole-like characteristics and habits, though these other voles tend to wander considerably further from water than the aquatic water vole. However, all will take a dip if the need arises.

THE MINK

Where mink are to be found, it would be safe to say that little else in the way of small mammals and water-birds would be anywhere in the vicinity, for this polecat-sized demon is possessed with a ferocity unequalled amongst our mammals and will kill viciously just for the sake of it.

Introduced into this country from America during 1929, to be bred for its valuable fur, escapees from farms soon colonized areas along the rivers of Devonshire. Since then they have become firmly established throughout southern England, parts of East Anglia, Wales, the Midlands and the lower reaches of Scotland. Whilst they have few enemies themselves, they will kill water birds, valuable fish and game to such a degree that now the Ministry of Agriculture has classified them as pests and declared all-out war on them.

Whilst the fur of farm-bred mink is valuable, that of feral (wild) mink is completely valueless so there is no incentive for hunters to expend much effort in trapping. The fur colour of the original wild mink is rich, glossy brown, but ranch minks can vary from white to pure black and this is reflected in the British wild mink.

Though a solitary, nocturnal animal, you might conceivably come across one during the daytime. Should you ever corner one by accident, make no attempt whatsoever to touch it, but instead get well away as quickly as you can for it will attack, showing no fear, and its razor-sharp teeth could inflict serious injury. Normally mink would disappear in a flash, long before you got too close, so although you should never put your arm down likely looking holes, don't worry unduly that one might spring out at you.

Nests are usually to be found in similar places to those frequented by the water vole and often the mink have eaten up the rightful owners.

Disappearing wild-life is usually an accurate pointer that mink have invaded an area.

THE COYPU

A danger to our economics, but for a different reason, the coypu is also classed as a pest. So serious is the damage they do that in the areas where they are found, trappers are employed who do nothing else but systematically and continuously kill these animals. During 1974 ten thousand of them were put down, yet still further efforts are needed.

I first saw this gigantic rodent when, as a lad of nine years, I was enticed into a fairground tent by a large notice declaiming *the largest rat in the world*. Three times I handed over my money, to stand in

Coypu. *Because they undermine river banks, causing them to collapse, they are classed as a serious pest.*

wide-eyed wonder at the spectacle of the *rat*, indeed many times larger than I had ever seen on the farm. My only feeling of disappointment, if my memory serves me well, came from the fact that it was not tearing at the bars of its cage but instead was placidly chewing a turnip. It was a number of years before I discovered how I and many others had been duped.

Coypu were imported into this country from South America for the same reasons and at the same time as the American mink and within a short time had followed the same pattern of escaping and colonising the surrounding districts. Their spread, however, has not been as dramatic and today they are mainly concentrated in the Broadlands, east and south of Norwich and the Suffolk coast.

A giant rat is not an unreasonable description of the coypu, but instead of sharp features they have blunt faces more like voles. A fully grown coypu is two feet long, has an eighteen inch scaly tail and can weigh up to as much as twenty pounds, though its average weight is about fifteen pounds. It has a large head, humped back and webbed feet, while like the otter its coat is completely waterproof. It is the underfur, known as *nutria*, which is valuable to furriers.

The main damage is caused by their burrowing habits, which often cause whole banks of rivers and dykes to subside. Also, as there is an estimated number of thirty thousand coypu, each capable of eating two pounds of greenstuff per day, the detrimental economic effect of this rodent on the countryside is spectacular. Their normal diet is roots of rush, reed and other aquatic vegetation. But they also eat cereals, kale and sugar beet, which they attack in June and July, nipping off the tops and killing the roots when it is too late for the farmer to re-drill.

Summer litters reach breeding age after three months; those born during the winter, after seven months. The average litter size is five, but as the young ones cannot survive on frozen food, for those born in the winter survival rate is low. However since 1969 we have had mild winters, therefore quicker breeding has been encouraged and at the same time a better rate of survival. The young are born in a nest of grass and marsh plants above water level. Being well developed at birth, they are able to move around immediately and within a few days can be seen swimming alongside the female. An interesting point here is the fact that the female's teats are situated high on the side of her body, unlike other mammals whose teats are underneath. The reason for this is to enable her young ones to feed without her leaving the water.

Young coypu fall prey to most carnivores, but as they reach their adult size, they can put up a formidable defence even to the extent of attacking a dog or man if provoked and as they possess typical rodent teeth and claws, but much magnified, the resultant injuries could be severe. The late autumn or early winter are good times to try to catch a glimpse of these strange animals, for vegetation is low and they tend to lessen their nocturnal habit somewhat in an effort to gain as much feeding time as possible before the winter proper arrives.

AUTUMN BIRD LIFE

Birds, too, are making the most of an abundance of food at this time, ever conscious of approaching hungry months. Early autumn, though, is largely a time of bird movement with the departure of many of our summer visitors and the arrival of those who flock daily to this country from colder lands to the north and east. Even our own residents seemingly affected by the general coming and goings, may be seen to change their quarters in surprisingly large numbers.

Although the departure of most of the summer visitors is delayed until autumn, some of them leave Britain as early as August. Among the first to go are adult cuckoos during July and August, leaving behind offspring who are still being reared by foster-parents, invariably species which do not migrate themselves. Swifts, though late arrivals, also like to get away early and this is possible because only having one brood, their nesting season is naturally considerably shorter; therefore both adults and young are ready for flight long before others who might have as many as three broods. The danger with those who have three broods – and swallows are an example of this – is that if the last family is reared too late, this in turn makes them late leaving this country and they run into extremely cold weather on their journey.

Whilst summer visitors are leaving, the gap they vacate is rapidly filled by winter visitors, though varieties of species are more limited. However, among the groups which do arrive may be included such

Dark Breasted Brent Geese

large and beautiful birds as swans, geese and ducks of various kinds. Two of these geese, the greylag and Canada geese, breed in the British Isles; none of the others do.

Among the more familiar of autumn newcomers are two foreign thrushes, redwing and fieldfare. Some of them may have arrived as early as July, but it is not usually until October that they become generally distributed. Fieldfares arrive in great flocks and remain here until April. Smaller than their relations, the mistle thrushes, they have very distinctive patches of grey on the head and rump. Fieldfares are often seen in company with other species of thrush, and their harsh *chacking* call soon identifies them. The redwing, a much smaller bird, has a thin, penetrating flight call and on October nights is as familiar as the lark in summer. The reddish colour on the sides of the bird helps to distinguish it when flying in a mixed flock. It is often interesting to count how many different breeds of thrush you can see flocking together. Our own native bird population is greatly augmented by the arrival in vast numbers of greenfinches, yellowhammers, tree sparrows and the bramblings or bramble finches. Bramblings are not unlike chaffinches in appearance while they are both wearing their winter plumage, but when they rise in flight the bramblings display a pale patch on the lower part of the back between the outstretched wings, a difference that cannot be noted while both breeds are moving to and fro on the ground pecking at beech-mast. Among the lesser-seen arrivals it is worth keeping a special eye open for interesting birds such as the siskins, redpolls, snow-buntings and great grey shrikes. The latter are larger than our own red-backed shrikes, though they share the same gruesome habit of impaling victims of their rapacious appetite on thorns until they are ready to eat them. This behaviour has earned them the name of *butcher birds*. A single thorny bush may be found adorned with the carcasses of rodents, large insects and small birds. The Latin name of the grey shrike, *exubitor* (sentinel), is derived from their habit of posting themselves on high twigs and other conspicuous places where they are able to keep a look out not only for their prey but for any member of the hawk family, a species against which the shrikes wage incessant war.

Shrikes are also competent mimics of the calls and songs of other birds, and the use of these powers is directed into lulling fledglings in their nests to think that their parents are approaching. The ensuing

Mallard *and dry reeds. Loose*

hungry racket they set up soon betrays their whereabouts to waiting shrikes, with fatal results for the young birds. The shrike call proper, is more like the gutteral *kew kew* of its enemy, the kestrel.

At this time of the year the cackling screech of jays will be heard in deep woodlands which never heard their cries during the summer months. The hedgerows ring with the fussy, piping song of the hedge-sparrow, while at night these same areas ring with the hunting calls of barn and tawny owl. In the woods the liquid notes of the song thrush have an autumnal solemnity about them and whilst the blackbird rarely sings, its *chinking* alarm note and frantic scuffling through fallen leaves warns every living creature in the vicinity that you are on your way. As you pass under coniferous trees you may be showered with falling cones or scales, which could be falling from the paws of squirrels or from the strangely-shaped beak of the crossbill. If you are unable to catch sight of the culprit, it is easy enough to tell which one is hiding above, for the squirrel nibbles off the scales to reach the seeds whilst the crossbill leaves them on.

As autumn advances, birds become more gregarious, moving together in great flocks that sweep up and down the fields and hedges as though guided by one mind. In large numbers around the coasts and marshes may be seen ducks and shovellers, mallard, teal, widgeon, tufted ducks and pochard; and by the end of October huge hoards of waders have reached our shores. Inland, our home-bred lapwings have been joined by many foreigners and, joining up with many species of gull, they may be seen swarming in clouds behind tractors, pecking at worms and grubs turned up by the plough. Particularly in the evening you will realize how large these congregations can be, as the birds all settle in one area to roost, but starlings always seem to collect together in greater numbers than any other species, often darkening the sky momentarily, as they swoop on woodlands with the precision of an army battalion, to weight down the branches and turn the ground below quite white with their droppings.

Many birds, while not sharing each other's company during the day-time, draw together as dusk approaches, so if you station yourself near a spinney which you know to be a roosting area, you could probably distinguish such species as sparrows, finches, wrens, tits, redwings, fieldfares and robins. Also at this time of night, you will be treated to a choral symphony, in every way as breathtaking as the dawn chorus, as each species tries to outdo its neighbour.

My particular favourites, with the exception of most birds of prey, are those birds which belong to the *corvidae* or crow family, a species which is more conspicuous at this time of year as they draw closer to man's bounty, whether in town or country. I cannot resist their impudent roguish ways or their buccaneering approach to life. What bird can equal the raven for its arrogant carriage, the jackdaw for mischievousness, or the jay and magpie for sagacity and cheek wrapped in bright plumage. To make up the numbers of birds grouped in this family I must add rook, carrion crow, hooded crow and the comparatively rare chough. Of this latter species there are less than seven hundred pairs remaining in Britain and of these the greatest majority are to be found in the slate quarries of Wales.

Unfortunately all men do not share my admiration for these feathered villains, though to be fair to fruit-growers, gamekeepers and farmers I must admit that I do not suffer any loss or damage from corvidae. Silent witness to this dislike may be found along certain fences abounding keepered property. There is a custom amongst gamekeepers of selecting a fence and thereafter using it as a *gibbet* upon which are hung the many and varied carcasses which fall to their guns, as trophies of their skill and watchfulness. Today, I would imagine these displays are purely for the gamekeeper's own satisfaction, but I suspect that in years gone by, probably his job depended not only on carrying out the work of killing suspected vermin, but that he was *seen* to be successful in his duties. On these gibbets you could find every member of the crow family, though not all of them deserve such a fate. Ranged alongside them you might also see in various stages of decay, the corpses of fox, stoat, weasel, mink, and occasionally owls, for even in this enlightened age some gamekeepers still shoot them.

THE RAVEN

To start at the top, as it were, let us look at our largest and most impressive crow, the raven. Once a familiar sight ranging up and down the streets of London, this species is now relegated to such areas as the mountainous districts of Ireland and Scotland, though they may occasionally be observed perched on cliff faces around the East and West coasts. Visitors to the Tower of London, however, may see the ravens which are retained there as traditional guardians of the Tower.

Ravens *can smell carrion from a mile away.*

Identification is simple, for at twenty-six inches in length they are some six inches larger than the carrion crow, which they resemble. Since the beginning of recorded time, ravens have been held in awe by the superstitious; not least of all for their supposed supernatural powers of foretelling death. This belief could have some factual basis, nothing to do with magic, for the raven's sense of smell is so acute that it can scent death from a mile away. In the same way as vultures, they seem able to tell when a sheep, for instance, is approaching death and they will fly in and settle down to wait for the end. Waiting is not always strictly observed, however, and often ravens and some of the other crows will peck out the eyes of a dying creature. They do not rely explicitly on carrion, but will prey indiscriminately on any creature they are capable of running down or overpowering, rabbits, hares, rats, mice, game of any kind, eggs, and even sickly lambs which they are perfectly capable of carrying away to their nests high in the rocky crags. Other than man, they have no enemies, for apart from being viciously strong, their nesting places are usually inaccessible. The golden eagle is our only resident larger than the raven and even they give the raven a wide berth, not so much from fear but because they become tired of being constantly harried whenever they fly too near a raven's nest, for no crow is more jealous of intruders, no matter whether they are large or small.

HOODED AND CARRION CROWS

For a long time it was thought that these two crows belonged to separate species, but as their only difference appears to be that the hooded crow has grey underparts and back, while the carrion is jet black, this has now been discounted; therefore they may be classed as one breed. Another point is that these two inter-breed freely, a state of affairs that does not exist with any of the other species of crow. Though we do have a two-way traffic either way, in the main, carrion crows are confined to more southern regions while the hooded or *hoodie* crow is its Scottish counterpart. Rather than write out both names, I will refer to both as *crow*. Non-countrymen are invariably confused between the crow and the rook, yet with a little observation the difference is easily told. Seen reasonably closely, rooks have a distinctive patch of white, bare skin at the base of the beak; crows heads are completely black. In flight rooks have a ragged appearance, again quite distinctive. Though not always true the traditional method of telling the two species apart is accurate nine times out of ten – flocks are rooks, and solitary or occasionally pairs are crows. Apart from appearance the two have little else in common, their habits being as different as chalk and cheese.

Crows are ubiquitous, and in heavily built-up areas where they have no fear of persecution, they are impudently tame. In this sort of environment they live up to their name and feed on whatever carrion or scraps meet their eye. But in the countryside they are the gamekeepers' deadly enemy. Breeding very early means that the crow is feeding a grown up family while other birds are still incubating eggs or feeding tiny fledglings, which rather suits their cannibalistic tendencies. Without mercy they will drive brooding birds from their nests and steal eggs or fledglings, undeterred by frantic cries from distressed parents. Screaming leverets will be taken from their mother's side and game chicks snatched from their hiding places. Newly born lambs are in constant danger for though they cannot carry them off like the raven, crows will kill and dismember them at leisure, flying backwards and forwards to their nest clutching gruesome parcels for the waiting young. With inherent cunning they are not foolish enough to leave tell-tale signs of their transgressions littering the ground beneath their nests and may be seen carrying animal debris some distance away from the site, so that attention is not drawn to their home. This is usually high in an inaccessible tree and composed of a rude bundle of sticks and roots, lined with some softer material. Like the raven, crows do not suffer intruders lightly and will attack any bird which approaches their domain, even their own offspring once they have left the nest.

THE ROOK

Though the broken bodies of rooks may be seen decorating the aforementioned gibbets, one can only hope that it is because of mistaken identity, for while doing practically no harm at all to man, they do a great deal of good. Rooks exist principally on corn and fruits, but their favourite foods are those which should endear them to man, for they eat beetles, larvae of beetles and many forms of insects and grubs which

Rooks *often colonize the same nesting sites for centuries.*

are injurious to crops. Hence they can most commonly be seen digging industriously in soft ground for food.

During winter rooks roost together in great flocks, usually not far from the *rookery* upon which they will descend during March, to prepare for the breeding season. Their nests are composed of an untidy bundle of twigs high in the branches of trees, set in open countryside. Young rookeries might only consist of a dozen pairs of birds, but some of them have been used for centuries and could contain up to seven or eight thousand. If you have never seen a rookery as large as this waking up at dawn, you have missed a spectacular sight, for as the rooks slowly rise in the air to form a great black cloud, you get the impression that every bird in the country is there before your eyes. Incidentally, it has been put forward that the phrase *as the crow flies* was coined in this way because the original observer was confused between crow and rook. When you give the matter some thought it is quite obvious, because when flying between two points, the crow will haphazardly meander across country whilst the rook will fly as though mapped on a course which may, in fact, be true, for as they wing their way back to the rookery from their feeding grounds, each rook will keep to this invisible pathway with hardly a deviation from the course set by the one in front.

THE JACKDAW

In many ways the jackdaw is like the rook, particularly in habits and feeding, though as most people are familiar with this cheerful perky bird confusion rarely arises. Having the same gregarious ways as the rook, it favours derelict buildings, or rock faces for its nesting places, rather than tall trees, though occasionally has no objections to taking over an abandoned rookery. A favourite habit of the jackdaw, however, is the one of stealing anything bright or attractive, as ornament for its nest. Although this sort of behaviour is quite common with many birds, particularly the crow family, it seems that the jackdaw has taken this hoarding instinct to the extreme.

The walk of the jackdaw is bright, almost chaplinesque, its movement quick and lacking the dignity which both the rook and the raven possess. In flight it is easily recognised by its rapid wing-beats and erratic flight pattern. A bird that seems to take more liberties than any of the other members of the crow family, it may often be seen sitting on the back of a sheep and apparently attacking it. This is not so, however, in fact what it is doing is feeding on the many ticks and other parasites which are embedded in the fleece or skin, thus doing the sheep a favour rather than harm. Starlings are another species which favour this type of mobile snack bar. The same behaviour might be observed on horses and cattle, but invariably this takes place early in the year, for they are bent on gathering hair to line their nests. Another clever habit, again shared with starlings, is the ability to mimic and jackdaws can easily be taught to talk if acquired early enough, but bear in mind that it is against the law to keep a wild bird which has not been bred and reared in captivity. These birds would have a ring placed on their leg shortly after hatching, to prove they are within the law.

JAY AND MAGPIE

In spite of the combined efforts of farmers and gamekeepers, who are prepared to shoot either bird at sight, you cannot go very far before encountering these handsome crows, for even against weighted odds they seem to thrive and multiply. This is due to an intelligent cunning, tempered with caution, plus the fact that they never seem to do anything without giving their actions some forethought.

The jay is a woodland bird which does make it rather difficult to see, for its beautiful colouration although bright, particularly on the wings, helps to camouflage it amongst the trees rather than make it conspicuous. The nest could best be described as a large blackbird's nest, with sticks for foundations and small roots for lining, but as it is usually very well concealed, though never very high in the branches of low trees, it is hard to find unless you follow the bird home. Apart from a great liking for fruit of all kinds with perhaps peas and beans to ring the changes, the jay is an accomplished egg thief, particularly from woodland ground nests like those of the partridge or pheasant. Fledglings too are killed and eaten, which does rather explain why such a pretty bird as this can be seen hanging lifeless from gamekeepers' gibbets. Though not as gregarious as rooks, jays are sociable birds and during the greater part of the year will be seen at least in twos or threes. In the springtime breeding season they congregate together, sending their raucous, unconnected cries ringing through the woods.

The magpie seems to have all the worst faults of the other crows, yet this is hard to imagine when watching it, for it appears so inquisitively friendly and harmless. Yet the magpie, too, is a stealer of eggs and young birds, grain, fruit and, like its larger relatives, will peck out the eyes of weak and sickly animals and tear them to pieces. A bird that is not frightened of approaching close to man's buildings, it will also attack chicks, ducklings and other domestic game. Apart from such unlawful diet, it also eats carrion, slugs, frogs, small rodents, grubs and a certain amount of harmful insects, though not in great enough numbers to balance the scales against the damage it causes elsewhere.

As adept in the art of thieving, as the jackdaw, there is little chance of you being able to see how intricately the nest is decorated with any sparkling objects which it can steal, for its home is invariably high in a tall tree. The nest is easily found and recognised, for it is a curious structure, large and obvious even from a distance. In the fork of a stout branch, a base is laid composed of thick twigs interlaced and glued together with mud. From this platform the sides are built up with thorny twigs and fibrous roots, extending up and over to form a roof, the whole structure usually being some two feet across. A single wide entrance hole is left in one side and the interior is lined with soft roots. Even if the nest were accessible, which it rarely is, the construction itself is a prickly deterrent to would-be egg collectors.

Though the magpie appears to be simply black and white, were you to examine one closely you would see that the black is shot with a beautiful greenish blue metallic lustre. However, apart from its colour, the most notable characteristic is its appearance whilst flying. Although the wings may seem to be abnormally short, in fact they have a span of twenty-seven inches as befits a bird thirteen inches in length, and the illusion of shortness is caused by our attention being diverted to the exceptionally long tail. A tail which, if you observe a magpie feeding on the ground, will be seen to jerk up and down spasmodically in a similar way to that of a blackbird's. Like the jay, magpies are sociable but not gregarious, but this social habit is not confined strictly to their own kind, for they may often be seen in the company of rooks, jackdaws and common crows, all of whom seem to accept them as hangers on.

THE CHOUGH

As stated earlier the chough is now rare in Britain. From a distance it can scarcely be distinguished from a jackdaw, but a closer examination soon reveals the difference in that the chough has bright scarlet legs and a long curved, scarlet bill. Whilst having the same inquisitive, perky but wary characteristics of the rest of the tribe, it lacks their damaging, rapacious habits, feeding mainly on insects, seashore offal and occasional grain. So it is strange and sad that the least offensive of corvidae should be the one which is so scarce.

THE HEDGEHOG

Whatever your age, if you are a comparative beginner in the art of nature observation, you can practise your skills on what must be our most easily seen mammal – the hedgehog.

The hedgehog is a creature of both town and country, where it may be seen at all times of the day. However, it is usually most active from

A **Hedgehog** *in the garden soon clears out unwelcome slugs and snails.*

dusk until dawn, when the slugs, snails and worms upon which it chiefly feeds come out from their hiding places in great numbers. It will also eat lizards, frogs, snakes and small rodents, while, like many other mammals it preys heavily on the eggs of ground-nesting birds, putting itself in the category of animals disliked by gamekeepers. An egg taken by a hedgehog is not smashed; instead a small hole is made in the shell through which the contents are drunk. In a similar manner it makes a hole in the centre of a snail's shell and eats the snail, without damaging the outermost structure. A story, often put down as an old wives' tale, is that hedgehogs suck milk from the teats of cows while they are lying down. Far from laughing at this as traditional nonsense, I would think that there is every likelihood that this does take place. The hedgehog, on an early morning tour of inspection for food must frequently encounter somnolent cows in a state of readiness for milking. It seems only logical that the hedgehog would grasp the opportunity of such an effortless meal!

This little creature's great liking for milk can be taken advantage of if you wish to entice a hedgehog to your back door, for if you know they pass through, or actually live in your garden, a saucerful placed outside every night will act as a guarantee. It will only take a couple of nights before they make a habit of calling and in fact may often arrive before you have a chance to place the food out. If your garden has plenty of low growing vegetation or trees and bushes under which leaves are allowed to accumulate, then it would be an ideal situation for hedgehogs to set up home. From October until early April they hibernate, buried deeply in piles of leaves, so should you inadvertently disturb one, make sure you cover it over with a thick covering of leaves or moss before leaving it to continue its sleep. If the weather becomes really cold, hedgehogs, in common with bats, will wake up and move around in search of food as protection against freezing to death, though as our winters rarely reach sub-zero temperatures, this does not often happen.

Though covered in prickly spines, you will find that you can pick up a hedgehog with your hands held flat, without any discomfort. But here a word of warning. They are invariably infested with fleas which, while they would not make a permanent home on you, would be quite happy to spend a few days, showing gratitude for your hospitality by biting you every now and again. If you are going to make a pet of a hedgehog the answer is to buy a suitable flea powder from your local pet shop or chemist and give it a liberal dusting. By use of the term *pet* I do not mean that you should imprison it in any way. Instead you should gain its trust by regular feeding, then you will find you have a permanent guest without the need of a wire cage. Apart from fleas, hedgehogs usually have a number of ticks clinging to the skin around their head. These are grey-coloured, oval-shaped, bloodsucking insects ranging from bead size to as much as small finger nail size. If you pull one off, the biting head remains in the skin to cause a festering sore, so what you have to do is get the tick to release its hold, and this is done by painting a drop of TCP, methylated spirits, or petrol onto its back. This method is worth bearing in mind, for often dogs pick up these unwholesome creatures and would require the same treatment.

At the approach of danger, real or supposed, the hedgehog crouches low or curls up into a tight ball, although they are quite capable of standing fully erect on all four legs and, indeed, look most comical when running like this at surprisingly high speeds, for they appear as though they have hitched up their skirts to gain extra speed. The curling up habit is the reason for so many of them being run over by cars, for as headlights approach, they make no effort to run away, but instead curl up in the middle of the road as their only means of defence. Their spines too, are of little defence against some of our more ferocious predators, though normally hedgehogs are left alone, being attacked

Hedgehog

only when food is really scarce or hard to find. Foxes have been known to roll them into water where, forced to uncurl, they become easy prey. Badgers seem unaffected by the spines, probably due to their own very tough feet and claws, usually skinning hedgehogs expertly, turning them inside out like a pair of discarded gloves, starting from the unprotected underparts. Stoats, weasels and mink are all able to break through the hedgehog's spiny barricade and gypsies, who regard them as a delicacy, roll them up in a ball of clay and cook them in the glowing embers of a fire. Add to this gamekeepers and motor cars, and you will see that the comparatively harmless hedgehog has a struggle to survive.

Mating takes place between March and July, so from May until September you may be fortunate enough to see families of three or seven youngsters waddling along behind mum. Better still, if you have been regularly feeding an adult pair, there is every chance that the young ones will be brought to your doorstep, perfect miniatures of their parents.

WINTER'S APPROACH

As November approaches, preparations for the coming of winter are almost complete, though this would depend to a certain degree on the weather in different localities. The hedgehog, insulated against the cold by a thick layer of fat, has buried itself under a pile of dead leaves, into the warmth of ground ivy, or disappeared into the depths of a disused rabbit burrow. Bats have hidden themselves away in hollow trees, under the eaves of buildings or among the rafters or thatch of roofs. Here their body temperatures sink to that of their surroundings and their heartbeats and breathing become weak and irregular. Dormice usually begin their winter sleep early in October, forsaking summer nests, which are loose balls of wide bladed grasses situated in low branches or brambles, for warmer winter nests underground or inside hollow trees. Though not a recommended treatment, it is quite possible to pick up a sleeping dormouse and examine it minutely without waking it, so deep is its sleep.

These three mammals are the only species in Britain which truly hibernate, though as mentioned before this winter sleep does not mean complete unconsciousness for the whole period, for it would be possible to see any one of these at some point during the period September till April.

For all our wild creatures the problems of surviving the long winter months are many, not least of all the general lack of food. Many do not succeed, dying from cold and hunger or just not waking from their hibernation. Those that do survive are the fittest and strongest of each species, which is nature's way of ensuring that only the most suitable are ready to breed subsequent generations in the following spring.

A **Harvest Mouse** *peers from its beautifully cylindrical nest.*

WINTER

Winter – to many of us this word conjures up mental pictures of cold bleak days, or more often, images of pending Christmas log fires and crisp snow. But what does it mean to birds, insects, animals and plants?

During November the wild flowers of summer and autumn continue to retreat before the oncoming winter. In fact, by the time this month is coming to an end the majority of them have vanished from sight.

Winter Aconite

PLANTS IN WINTER

The actual date when a plant ceases to flower depends almost entirely on the weather and unless this is particularly severe you should still be able to gather a colourful and interesting collection of wild flowers on any country walk. White campion, red clover, yarrow, wild pansy, corn marigold, creeping buttercup and devil's-bit scabious are but some of those which you may find. Plants which have apparently *died* are not finished for ever. In the case of annuals, while the plant itself has perished, its very hardy seeds live on, capable of surviving the most extreme weather. On the other hand perennial plants retire into their bulbs or corms, where, underground and protected from frosts and snows, they wait out the winter. Some perennials, like snowdrops and crocus, not only sprout but send up flowering shoots long before spring arrives.

Very common in December are a number of so-called annuals which often survive the winter as individuals. Shepherds purse, groundsel and chickweed are typical examples of these plants. They seem to have no real resting season at all, and if circumstances are favourable, they produce a continuous succession of generations all the year around. During December you may find a number of wild flowers which are stragglers from earlier months. How many types you will identify depends again on the weather, so will obviously vary from year to year. In mild seasons you will have little difficulty in finding the lingering blossoms of such plants as charlock, wild radish, lady's mantle, sandworth, together with speedwell, dandelion and yarrow.

BUDS

Deciduous trees, stripped of their summer greens and autumnal tints, stand bare and exposed, save for withered leaves, discoloured galls and and the husks of their fruits. Although they may appear to be devoid of life, they are in fact very much alive, as you will find upon examination of their winter buds, which are characteristic of each and every species. As protection against frosts and rain, winter buds are closely covered with firm, tight fitting scales and if you strip back this hard outer coat you will find pale but living green. Early in the winter this living green

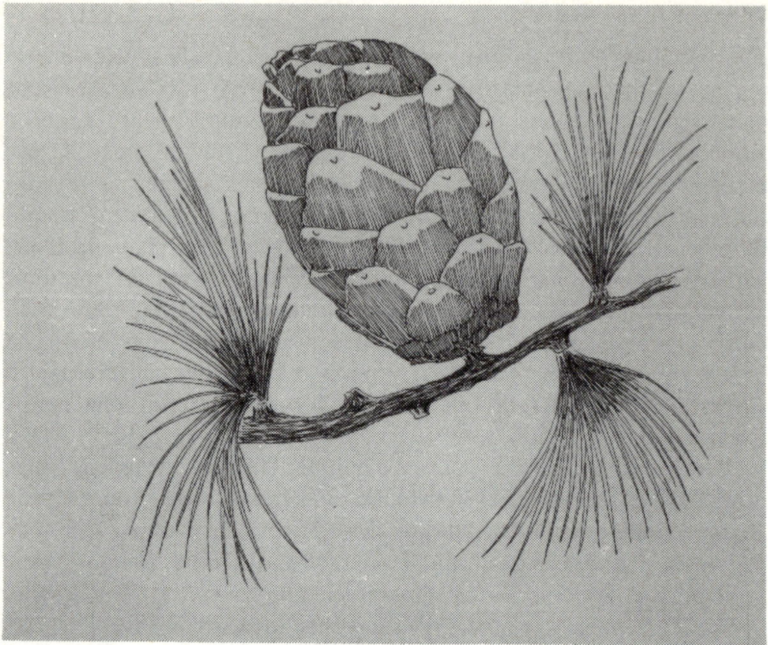

Larch *cone*

has no particular shape and pattern and in fact for a couple of months nothing at all happens within the dormant bud. Then the bud begins to swell and lengthen and if you cut one open at this stage you will find that the shapeless green has started to take on the form of tiny leaves.

Probably the best known bud is that of the horse chestnut, for its bulbous shape and toffee-like stickiness, seem to have a fascination for everyone. Yet all trees have buds which are equally attractive and always peculiar to the species. The jet black, velvet covered buds of the ash are easily recognised, as also are the long pale brown and pointed buds of the beech. Others may be short and stout, or long and cylindrical, green, brown, grey, in fact there are such a profusion of varieties that you could spend many interesting hours finding and identifying them.

There are few of us who do not feel a great affection, almost respect, for trees; venerable outgrowths, some of which started life as seedlings while wolves and wild boars roamed the countryside. Wintertime then, is the season in which you can see the true identity, general shape and structural beauty of trees, a sight which is half concealed by foliage during the greater part of the year. It would be true to say that for those interested in trees, their season should begin not in spring, but now while bole and branches are clearly defined.

The mental picture of the seasons which most people carry in their minds are invariably quite detached from the reality. For instance, summer is not one long season of balmy days with larks singing high in the blue while myriads of flaming butterflies cluster around gaudy flowers. Neither is autumn full of peaceful golden days; often it is a period when we have frightening storms. Similarly winter is not an endless period of grey days and colourless landscapes. Although tints may be subdued there is still an abundance of colour, sometimes in unexpected places.

HOLLY AND THE IVY

Various berries supply much of this colour and generally the most prolific are those of the holly. Fortunately for those of us who use it as traditional decoration at Christmas, its berries are unripe and bitter tasting to the palates of birds, otherwise they would strip the trees and bushes bare long before our festive season. Once ripe, however, the bright red fruits soon form a high proportion of the diet of pigeons, thrushes, starlings and many other birds. It is because the holly tree wishes its berries to be eaten that they are so juicily attractive. Swallowed whole, it is not long before the hard indigestible seed held within the pulpy fruit is passed out in the birds' droppings to germinate far away from the tree. Incidentally, holly trees are either male or female, and though both bear attractive white flowers in May, it is only on the female tree that these develop into red berries.

To resist water loss when the soil is iron hard, in the grip of winter frosts, holly has leaves which are thick and waxy. This explains why it does not wither when adorning our walls at Christmastide.

Now for a poser. If you were shown two holly leaves and asked to point out which one of these came from the bottom of the tree and which came from the top, do you think that apart from the picker, you or anyone else could possibly know? After all, you might say, one leaf looks just like another. With most trees one leaf does look like all the others, but with the holly tree nature has given it protection and at the same time supplied a simple answer to the question. During winter it is the only broad-leaved tree with green, nourishing foliage, and it follows that browsing deer and other herbivores would soon strip the lower boughs. To prevent this happening the leaves lower down on the tree are protected by tough, sharp spines, a deterrent for any animal. Higher up where they cannot be reached you will find the leaves smooth edged and utterly spineless.

The ivy, another traditionally *Christmasy* plant is one which also adds a splash of colour to otherwise leafless woods and rides. Whilst various plants may vie for the title of first flower of the year, indisputably the flower, or flowers, of the ivy are the last to bloom. Reversing the order of normal seasonal growth, it bears flowers from the late autumn, and berries during spring. There is an interesting comparison between the leaves of ivy and the leaves of holly, for as well as having leaves that are smooth and waxy to prevent water loss, the ivy also has two different shapes of leaf on the same tree. In its young state, ivy has a fleshy stem and bears the familiar lobed leaves. Dressed in this foliage it grows along the ground, woodland floor, or hedgerow base until it reaches an upright surface to which it can attach itself. Once it has attained a reasonable height, and this can vary depending upon the height of its *ladder,* its adolescence gives way to adulthood; now the upper leaves lose their lobes and become quite smooth edged, whilst at the same time the ivy begins to bear flowers and fruits.

While in its juvenile stage and growing along the ground, do not confuse this common ivy with another plant which goes by the misleading name of ground ivy. The latter is neither related nor in any way similar to the common ivy. In fact, it is a pretty creeping plant, with square stems and leaves that are heart-shaped and arranged in pairs. These leaves are coloured and textured like those of the hop plant, which is not surprising, for long before the hop plant was cultivated in the fifteenth century, ground ivy served the same purpose in the brewing of beer, namely that of clearing and flavouring.

Common ivy has a rather undeservedly bad reputation for killing off the trees upon which it climbs, hence you may often come across ivy plants with their very thick woody stems severed at the bottom, which is the work of farmers or foresters. Ivy is not a parasite in the true sense, nor does it strangle its host. It uses fellow trees purely for support. There are two ways in which it might be harmful. The first, I suspect only to a trivial degree, is that the underground roots deprive the host tree of water and soil nutrients. The second does give rise to the fallacy that it can strangle a tree, for when it has climbed one hundred feet, grown a trunk or stem as thick as a man's leg and spread itself over every branch, then its sheer weight could very likely bring down the host tree.

Berries of **Mountain Ash**

MISTLETOE

Definitely a real parasite, though not a dangerous one, is the mistletoe, the real spirit of romantic Christmas. Many people must imagine that this plant is cultivated, for they never come across it other than in a florist's window, accompanied by an exorbitant price tag.

Mistletoe grows only in southern Britain and in these areas it is by no means rare. It may appear hard to find to the casual observer, however, as it is usually hidden high in the fork of a branch.

Its berries, which ripen during winter, are soft, white and very sticky. Birds who eat this fruit find that having finished their meal the hard seeds adhere to breast feathers, beaks and feet. Flying off to another tree they carefully preen themselves and in the process wipe off the seeds on to convenient branches. Mistle thrushes are only one species among many which enjoy this fruit. Should the bird wipe the seed on to a fir tree or an elm tree, for instance, nothing happens because the mistletoe is fussy as to where it likes to grow. But if they choose an apple, pear or poplar tree, then some days later the seed puts out a tentative sucker and anchors itself firmly to the branch. Next comes a tiny rootlet, which must be as tough as a drill, for slowly it pierces the bark and grows downwards into the living tissue of the tree. Bear in mind that this takes place during the winter, so the host tree is lying dormant with no sap flowing through its branches. However, once having gained a foothold, the tiny mistletoe seed is content to follow the example of its host and lie dormant until spring.

As soon as the host tree begins to send sap surging through its branches in early spring, the mistletoe seedling puts up a pale green shoot, while its roots push further and further into sap filled tissue, to feed on the water which the tree has sent up for the use of its own shoots and buds. However, the amount the mistletoe *taps* off is so minute that it hardly, if ever affects the tree. As time goes on, branches develop and divide repeatedly until the mistletoe bush grows often as large as four feet across. Once established, these bushes, high in the branches of an alien tree, last for as long as ten years or more. Berries appear in the following winter.

So far I have mentioned flowering plants, yet everywhere in town and country, you can always find many, many species of non-flowering plants, which are often minute, usually inconspicuous and invariably overlooked. Under this heading come simple plants known as lichens, mosses, algae and fungi. These plants provide a great deal of colour, though you might have to get quite close to many of them to appreciate this fact.

LICHENS

Most of you are probably familiar with at least one member of the lichen family. By familiar I mean that, broadly speaking, you know that what you are looking at is definitely a lichen. The most commonly known are those which grow on trees in hair-like tangles, their colours varying from pale grey, green and orange. This type of lichen, though well known by sight, does not have a common name; in fact, very few of the one thousand, three hundred and fifty five species of lichens do have common names, and are referred to by botanists by their latin names only.

Many of the others, although equally familiar by sight, are not always recognised as lichens, but are thought of as some kind of nasty mould or rot.

The curious thing about lichens is that they are not one individual plant, but are a combination of a fungus and thousands of microscopic plants from the algae group. Neither one is a parasite on the other, for each supplies a definite need. The fungus part fixes the plant to a suitable surface and collects the moisture so vital to algae growth; it also protects the algae and determines the various shapes of the eventual lichen. In return, the algae cells contain chlorophyll, and manufacture sugars which the fungus feeds on. This mutual aid society enables lichens to grow where no other plant could survive.

Lichens do not have roots but absorb water and nutrient gasses through their upper surfaces, therefore they are very sensitive to atmospheric pollution. For this reason you are unlikely to find them growing in heavily built up areas, where industrial wastes and heavy traffic despoil the air. In clean areas, lichens are very common. They may be found in the woods and lanes, on heaths and windswept moors, along the sea-shore and high on mountain tops. They cover old walls and paths, spread themselves over tile and slate roofs, they grow in tufts from the branches of trees or hang down in ragged festoons, taking up many and varied shapes. Some are like crumpled ferns, some like intricate rosettes whilst others look like horses' tails, heavily lobed seaweed or, in some cases, like patches of coal black tar.

So taken collectively, they make a beautiful spectrum of colour, turning the usual drab surfaces they grow upon into pretty shades of grey, silver, green, yellow, red and bright orange.

Of the few lichens that do have *popular* names you might look out for the wreaths of crinkly pale grey *necklace moss*, usually found growing on well-established fir or oak trees. Another is the conspicuous *club moss* that grows in clusters of tiny grey-green cups on damp banksides or fallen trees. This type is related to the *reindeer moss*, a lichen of heaths, moor and mountainous places. These are greyish-white, and grow tangled among heathers and low growing scrubs. In Lapland this is the staple diet of reindeer, for it can grow in the bleak northern parts where other plants cannot survive. Britain's own small herd of reindeer, introduced into the Cairngorms, also feed on this lichen, scraping away thick coverings of snow with their broad hooves in order to reach it.

The above names are an instance of where popular names can throw one off the scientific track, as it were, for though called cup moss, reindeer moss, etc, they are not mosses, nor are they in anyway related.

MOSSES

Real mosses are individual small green plants which rarely grow more than a few inches high and are common wherever they can retain moisture. During the winter, mosses are at their brightest and greenest. Yet even if they become completely dried out during the summer, the first shower of rain restores and revitalizes them, and their green returns as if by magic.

The areas where mosses can be found are as varied as those of the lichens. For every type of habitat, there is a species of moss. On the banks of streams and sides of ditches, grows the delicately beautiful *feather moss*, so-named because while numbers of these plants grow in a tangle together, individually each one resembles a soft pale green feather. On boggy ground you will invariably see large clumps of *goldilocks*. At first glance, this moss appears to be covered with golden star-like flowers, but on closer examination these *flowers* turn out to be just bunches of leaves crowded together in tiny rosettes. Incidentally, while mosses have stems and leaves, they do not have flowers. Like ferns and fungi they reproduce by way of spores or, alternatively, by small pieces breaking off the main plant to form another plant.

Wherever there has been a bonfire one can guarantee that sooner or later will spring up yellow-green patches of a moss that is quite unique among the six hundred species we have in Britain. This preference for growing on sites of fires has earned it the name of *charcoal burner*. During dry weather its stalks curl up tightly, then when rain returns they straighten out.

Similar to the lichens, very few mosses have *popular* names, so I cannot give you any easy to remember references and would not wish to burden you with a list of latin tongue-twisters. If you wish to make a serious study of mosses, then there are many publications which deal exclusively with this subject. However not knowing a plant's name does not detract from its visual beauty.

Though very primitive, mosses make a valuable contribution to plant life. They can grow on the poorest of soil or where no soil exists at all, which are places where more sophisticated plants cannot possibly thrive. As they grow and spread over the ground the older moss plants die and crumble away, while fresh green moss is constantly springing up to replace them. After a few years, a gradually thickening layer of fine nutritious mould is formed. In this the seeds of flowering plants can germinate and, in turn, spread and add to the layer of humus, turning what was once barren into fruitful ground.

Sphagna or bog mosses are easily recognised as a group, for they are all basically of the same form, namely, large raised cushions with dense clusters of tiny leaves, varying in colour from green to dark red. These mosses make up the bogs of north and west, for their stems and leaves hold water like sponges. Large beds of rich peat are formed as the mosses grow layer upon layer, year after year, on top of their own decaying stems. When solidly compressed after many years this forms the peat which is still used in place of coal in some areas. Because this moss is so absorbent, nurserymen use it as a moist bandage to wrap round the roots of plants which they wish to send over long distances.

ALGAE

Now we come to *algae* the simplest and most primitive of all plants. These are normally totally ignored, or cursed for the discolouration they cause on damp walls.

Algae grows wherever there is moisture; on land, in freshwater and in the sea where it might be green, red, brown or blue. However, regardless of its main colour, it always contains green chlorophyll. This is a substance which, coupled with sunlight, enables plants to manufacture their own food from water and carbon-dioxide. Known as photosynthesis, this process has a very valuable by-product – oxygen. Conversely, the by-product of our own breathing system is carbon-dioxide. So you can see that plants are not on this earth simply for us to eat or to look at, but to recycle our waste and, in return, give us fresh air.

The most obvious algae in Britain are the single celled type which grow in powdery, bright green profusion on damp walls, roofs, and generally on the north faces of trees, a point to remember if you have left your compass at home. The green film seen on these surfaces is made up of millions of individual microscopic plants, which makes it hard to believe that they are closely related to a seaweed, which grows in the Pacific to lengths in excess of six hundred feet.

Other algae which live in fresh or seawater are known as plankton, which is simply a word of Greek derivation meaning *that which wanders.* Plants which are swept backwards and forwards at the whim of the currents are called *phytoplankton.* Animals which live in a similar style are known as *zooplankton* and this name also applies to *those that wander* in the air, such as aphids and minute spiders which fly on silken threads, often as high as twenty-five thousand feet.

These microscopic algae – plankton – are a major source of food for most aquatic life; even the massive blue whale lives entirely on these plants which it sieves from the sea water. All seaweeds are algae, though it is difficult to relate the many and varied shapes, colours and sizes of seaweeds to the well-known powdery algae. In freshwater, confusion may also arise, for some of the higher algae like the stoneworts, of which there are thirty species, are so large and complex in comparison that they resemble aquatic flowering plants proper.

The single celled algae seem to have a liking for striking up partnerships with other plants or animals. I have mentioned the dual role played by algae and fungi, their end product being lichen. But there are other combinations known as symbiotic partnerships. This is where the algae live inside the bodies of aquatic animals such as freshwater sponges, tiny relations of the jellyfish, known as hydra, and in the funnel shaped single celled stentor. Both parties benefit. The algae gain carbon-dioxide and other wastes from their host, while the latter gains a rich supply of oxygen.

An amusing colonization is that of the algae which live upon the South American sloth. The hair of the sloth is peculiar in that it is very coarse and grooved. The plants live and grow in these grooves though to no apparent benefit to themselves. However, the slow moving animal benefits considerably in that it is well camouflaged from its enemies by being turned green by the algae and becoming virtually invisible among the trees in which it lives.

FUNGI

Lastly we come to the fungi, which are non-flowering plants. Most people associate the word *fungi* with toadstools, yet this term covers a wide range of plants which include mildews, yeasts, rusts, moulds and other plant and animal diseases. To qualify as a fungus a plant must be non-flowering and lacking in chlorophyll, the green matter mentioned previously which helps other plants to produce food by aid of sunlight. Lacking this important ingredient, fungi have to rely on organic matter derived from both dead and living plants and animals. Those types which feed on living substances are known as parasites; those which feed on dead matter are called saprophytes.

I will deal here, briefly, with the fungi popularly known as toadstools, as the others are really outside the scope of this book, fascinating though they are, and certainly worth pursuing in more technical publications.

Fungi grow from spores, not seeds, and an interesting experiment may be carried out by carefully plucking the fruiting body or cap of a variety of species and laying them, pores down, on a piece of clean white paper. If you leave them overnight, in the morning upon lifting the caps, you will discover that thousands of spores have fallen onto the paper making an imprint of the underneath of the cap. Each species will have a different pattern and may be labelled and *fixed* to the paper by gently spraying them with any aerosol hair lacquer or varnish.

As an example, a mushroom measuring one inch across will normally drop between four or five million spores. Vast though this number may seem, only a tiny proportion of them find suitable ground in which to germinate. Those spores which do find acceptable conditions send out very fine threads which branch and intertwine. In this tight mesh of threads small knobs appear which soon begin to enlarge, push their way up to the surface and eventually pop out of the soil as the fungi fruits or toadstools.

Many of these fungi are edible, though in Britain only the cultivated mushroom is eaten in any quantity. In an earlier section I have pointed out the dangers of assuming that certain fungi are edible, but with no apologies I will stress the fact once more. It is essential to learn to recognise the many different species, for none of the generally accepted tests to distinguish between poisonous varieties are of any value whatsoever. For instance, a misconception widely held is that edible mushrooms are easily recognised, not only by sight, but by the way in which you can peel the skin from the cap with little or no effort. As a young boy I blindly accepted this myth as a fact, but since then I have peeled many varieties, most of them poisonous, so I am now a great deal wiser on this score. The mushroom does have a poisonous counterpart, which in many ways is similar in appearance. A clue to its effect if eaten comes from its name *death cap*. So be on the safe side and leave them alone.

Though most fungi fruit in autumn, you can find many colourful varieties right through the winter. A few examples being the beautifully red, white-spotted, fly agaric; the yellow, crocus-shaped chanterelle; saffron milk-cup, oyster fungus and the pale orange-yellow of the winter fungus. Many toadstools always grow in the same type of locations. For instance, the fly-agaric will, nine times out of ten, be found under beech trees. In fact beech woods are a popular place for many fungi, not only under the tree but actually growing on the tree, as in the case of tinder, black bulgar, oyster fungus and beech tuft. The lobe-shaped jew's ear fungus favours elder trees, while the bright orange witches

Fly Agaric *normally grows in the vicinity of beech trees.*

butter normally sticks (literally) to oak trees. So you can see that knowing where these species are likely to grow can be a great asset when searching them out.

Some fungi are quite beneficial to man and a remarkable instance of this may be found in the behaviour of a fungus which does not have a popular name, but can only be referred to as dactyella. This fungus traps and digests nematodes, commonly known as roundworms, which are the cause of various illnesses affecting horses, cows, pigs, man and some types of crops. On its underground stalks this helpful fungus grows tiny rings, formed from three cells, which stand up from the rest of the plant. When a roundworm noses its way into a ring, the cells swell up and the worm is caught like a rabbit in a snare. The fungus then grows into the body of the worm, digests and absorbs it.

Have you ever seen a *fairy ring* – those circles of dark green grass, usually found on close-cropped areas such as lawns, golf courses and grazing land? Superstition has it that they are caused by the twinkling feet of dancing fairies. However, at the risk of disillusioning those believers in the little people, the truth is somewhat less romantic. They are, in fact, formed by a fungus growing steadily outwards. As it advances, it brings about changes in the soil that lead to the liberation of nitrogen, and this in turn stimulates and makes richer the grass within the ring, thus producing a lush dark green zone. The circles increase in size as the fungus grows outwards at a rate of something like a foot per year, so, bearing this in mind, you will be able to calculate the age of the next ring you find.

During your winter walks if you keep your eyes open for all the aforementioned species, including lichens and algae, plus the thousands I have not mentioned, you will hardly notice the lack of wild flowers that would normally hold your attention during the greater part of the year.

Horn of Plenty Fungus

ANIMALS IN WINTER

Those mammals which hibernate throughout the winter months, are by now fast asleep in safe hiding places. It is often stated that these creatures are *tucked up warm*, yet in truth, while in this torpid state which is as close to dying as it is possible to get, body temperatures fluctuate with that of the surroundings. Should the temperature drop to a dangerous level, usually the mammal will wake and move around, though not too far from its chosen sleeping place. Hence during extremely cold weather, you may catch a glimpse of a hedgehog teetering through the snow, bats flitting across a frosty moon, or even a very thin looking dormouse peering at you from the bare stems of brambles.

Of the seventy species of mammal we have in the British Isles, only fourteen species hibernate, and twelve of these are the various species of bat. Apart from mammals, a great number of insects and backboneless creatures go into hiding, as do many backboned animals, such as frogs, toads, snakes and lizards.

Whilst many butterflies and moths pass the winter months in one of their earlier stages – either egg, caterpillar or pupa – a few hide up in dry sheltered places as adult winged insects. Brimstone, peacock and small tortoiseshell butterflies are examples, and if they manage to survive the winter, these and some other species may be seen on the wing very early in spring, or even on sunny days before winter is over.

The half joking question of *where do flies go in winter* often arises. Well, I don't know about them all, but last winter whilst repairing a roof, I had occasion to strip back the insulating felt covering the rafters. Underneath were literally hundreds upon hundreds of house flies, with an assortment of bluebottles and lacewings thrown in for good measure. Like the butterflies and moths, true flies (and this term covers some five thousand species in Britain) also pass through the winter in various stages – egg, large pupa or as adults – in the situations already described.

Whilst most air flying insects disappear from sight, and ground insects become virtually inactive, aquatic insects remain generally lively. During rough weather and hard frosts they may remain motionless for sometime, but on the whole, life underwater goes on undisturbed. Even when ponds and lakes are coated with ice, aquatic insects may still be

Orb Spider *spinning web.*

seen moving underneath, as can fish which prey on these insects, for they are also active throughout the winter.

Worms are creatures one would imagine to be the first into some underground hiding place, not to show themselves until spring is well under way. This is not so, for at most times during the winter you may come across them on the surface, usually at night, as this is when they mate. Often a sudden frost may catch many worms unawares making it impossible for them to retreat back into the frozen earth. Then, in the morning you will find them dead, enclosed in a thin sheath of ice; or occasionally you might find an empty tube of ice showing the marks of a worm's ringed body – evidence of a lucky escape. Normally, though, worms are aware of pending changes in the weather. Rain they love; frost, as I have already shown, they detest and at such times they retreat deep underground, where they lie knotted together in a tight mass. Slow-worms – no relation if you remember – also hibernate coiled in this manner, usually in places such as manure and compost heaps where a fair amount of heat is generated. Grass snakes and adders also go to sleep in groups, though they are not quite so gregarious as the slow-worm. Again compost heaps, haystacks and piles of leaf mould are favourite positions.

Frogs hibernate in the soft mud at the bottom of a pond or water-filled ditch. During this period they dispense with their lungs, and breathe solely by absorbing oxygen through the skin. Immature frogs do not live under water, instead they find a convenient hole on land in which to hide away, disused burrows, or martins' nests in clay banks being much-favoured locations. Toads and newts follow a similar pattern of behaviour.

For a long time it was thought that both the squirrel and the badger retired completely during the cold months, but it is now known that while they both spend long periods in their respective homes, they still venture out in all but the most inclement weather. Like many other mammals, they are able to go for days at a time without food, because during autumn when food was plentiful, they put on a considerable amount of fat and this helps them get through periods when it is not possible or desirable to find food.

Rabbits, on the other hand, are about in almost every kind of weather looking for food. When grass is buried under a layer of snow, they either dig down to it, or ignore it completely and turn their attention to peeling the bark from trees to reach the juicy cambium layer beneath, seriously damaging the trees in the process.

Because they are so common, having practically recovered from the effects of myxomatosis, rabbits tend not to excite too much interest on the part of ramblers and animal watchers. Yet they have a life style that is as complex and equally interesting as that of more sought after *finds* such as fox and badger. So next time you are out walking make a point of not only trying to *see* rabbits but of *observing* them, for a great difference lies between these two words. Obviously you cannot expect to learn very much of these complex habits from one or two casual observations, but I am sure that once you begin to watch rabbits, you will find that you will want to know more and more about them.

SOME FLESH EATING MAMMALS

At this point it would not be amiss for me to qualify the difference between animal and mammal. Simply, all living things which are not plants, are collectively known as animals, yet normally this term is popularly applied only to those creatures which are four-legged and furry; for example, dog, badger, squirrel and mouse, although these and others in the group should correctly be referred to as mammals. Under the main heading of animals, all life is classified into twenty-six major groups, of which twenty-five are made up of invertebrates, or creatures without backbones. Most of the more familiar animals belong to a sub-division of the remaining group, which contains animals with backbones such as fish, birds, mammals, reptiles and amphibeans.

Winter time, more so than any other season, is a time for hunter and hunted. While other types of food are in short supply carnivores tend to rely solely on a diet of meat, whereas at other times this is usually supplemented by at least a 50% diet of vegetable and insect food. The lack of dense undergrowth at this time of the year is a great help, for it allows us to catch sight of these hunting creatures. Also many of them virtually dispense with their nocturnal habit, for favourable weather conditions are at a premium. So you stand a much greater

Fox *scraping away snow to reach greenstuff or roots.*

chance of catching a glimpse during the afternoon of creatures which are normally night prowlers.

Carnivores, or flesh-eating mammals, may be seen in most parts of Britain. These animals, without exception, make no provision for the long winter months, so with them all it is a case of hunt and kill, or starve.

Of our four large carnivores, badger, otter, wild cat and fox, the latter is the one most likely to be seen on a casual basis, whether you happen to be walking in town or country. Town foxes tend more towards their traditional nocturnal habit than their country cousins, yet to see one as late as ten o'clock in the morning would not be exceptional.

However, no matter when or where you catch a glimpse of this fascinating animal, you will see for yourself that all the clichés normally applied to the fox are true, for its whole appearance is tailored towards being our most cunning, totally aware, sleek and nimble footed mammal, for its size.

A lengthy physical description of this well-known animal is hardly necessary, though one or two points are worth mentioning. A fox's colouring can be somewhat diverse from the accepted norm of russet upper parts, white chest and underparts, with black tipped ears and feet. Of the many foxes both dead and alive, which I have examined over the years, only 35% conformed to this traditional colour. The remaining percentage slid gradually down a colouration scale which ended with a small number that were black and white from the chest down. These *pied* fur foxes, while not an everyday occurrence, are by no means rare; in fact, throughout our birds and mammals these mutations may be found, blackbirds and rabbits being particularly prone to this variation.

To differentiate between dog fox and vixen (as the female is known) without a physical examination, is virtually impossible in the field. Many reference books state that the dog fox is bigger, thicker round the neck, and broad muzzled. Yet this has been contradicted on so many occasions, that it must be ignored. As I write, the mounted heads of two foxes glare down fiercely at me. This dog and vixen were unfortunately killed while crossing a motorway, side by side. The largest and most ferocious head, or mask, belongs to the female, while the small feminine looking head is that of the male.

The white tip, or tag, on the end of the brush, at one time was thought to signify the owner was male, but again this was an erroneous belief, for in some cases both sexes have it, whilst in others neither.

General dimensions vary considerably, for an adult fox can weigh from between eleven and fifteen pounds. Its body length may be from twenty-one to twenty-seven inches, and its brush length from eleven to seventeen inches. Yet of well over a hundred foxes I have measured, while everything else was inconsistent, the height from ground to shoulder rarely altered from just around fifteen inches.

The fox is not a creature of the night by choice, for many years ago it was as diurnal in habit as, for example, a squirrel is now. The most probable reason for their change in habit was that the general persecution of rabbits, mice etc, by themselves and other predators, drove this natural prey into the seclusion of darkness – hence they had to follow. The nocturnal habit confers many advantages, the main one being that hunting is greatly facilitated because scent and sound are more readily conveyed at night.

A fox's eyes alone suggest that diurnity and nocturnality come and go as ecological expedients suggest, for unlike the owl, which is wholly of the night and virtually blind in daylight, the fox is equally at home in either medium.

A walk in most woodlands will let you discover, if not always the animal itself, at least much evidence of its *activity*. Shallow scrapings in the soil indicate where a fox dug for hidden bulbs or roots. The neatly severed wing or tail feathers of some luckless bird tell their own story. While rufous hairs, snagged on barbed wire, might well give you a clue to some fox's normal runway. Along these paths you will find droppings, and these are easily identified for they are roughly three inches long, twisted and always sharply tapered at both ends. A closer examination of these droppings will reveal bone remains, beetle wings' cases and a fair amount of hair, much in the same way as an owl's pellet, which I will detail later.

Wintertime, by giving us an abundance of soft mud, supplies the perfect medium for recording those animals which have passed by. However, you will have to look for prints quite closely, for unless in snow they are not always obvious.

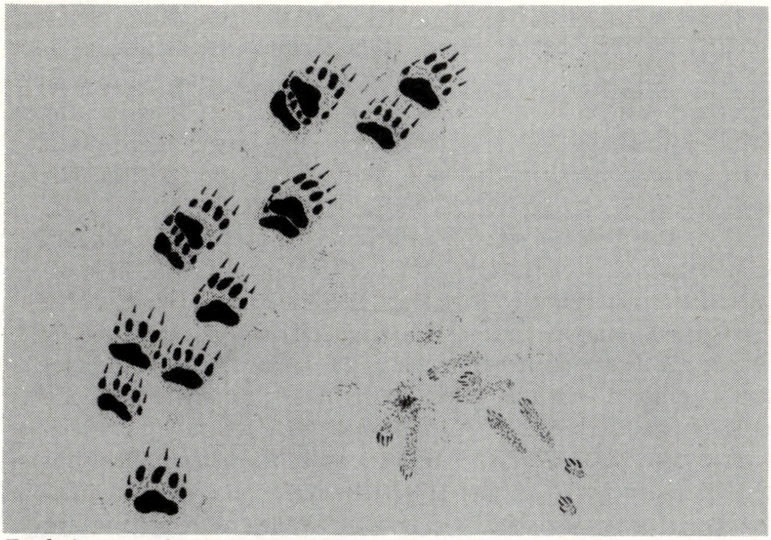

Tracks in snow of **Badger** *and* **Rabbit**

A fox's footprint is easily distinguished from that made by a domestic dog, the chief distinctions being that a fox's pad is small and triangular shaped, with four toe marks arched tightly around it, while the print also has a tendency for the two central toes to point inwards. A dog's print, on the other hand, has a toe pattern that is generally wide spread, although the pad size will vary between different breeds. In really soft mud, a fox's print shows hair traces between toe and pad, whereas a dog's print does not.

The general line of the track can also help you differentiate, for when trotting, a fox follows a purposeful course; a dog rarely does, but instead tends to be erratic with frequent pauses and detours.

The fox is virtually omnivorous, but in the main its basic diet consists of small rodents, beetles, worms, carrion and vegetable matter, or in fact anything that is locally predominant depending on the season. The stomach contents of one fox I examined at the height of the fruit season revealed nothing else but Victoria plums. Foxes will kill chickens, sickly lambs and old cats given the opportunity, but if other food is readily available they are less of a threat to livestock than dogs, who have been estimated to kill ten thousand sheep per year.

By no means silent throughout the year, the fox tends to be heard more during the breeding season, as the receptive vixen calls loudly for suitors. This takes place during December and January. The shrill yapping scream echoing through the dark night can bring as many as five dog foxes to the vixen's side, though only one will be accepted as a mate, leaving the others circling round, scuffling and fighting amongst themselves.

Once mated the pair select a breeding den or *earth*, which is normally an enlarged rabbit burrow, and prepare for the birth of the litter which will occur some fifty-two days later. The litter usually consists of four, grey-coated youngsters, blind and completely dependent on the vixen. By the tenth day their eyes open and they have most of their teeth, though probably not the molars, and a hint of gingery fur is beginning to show around the head. At four weeks they are quite foxy looking and are ready to leave the earth for periods. From then until the autumn the vixen teaches them the art of survival, upon which the family breaks up, each going their separate way. As the breeding season arrives these cubs are sexually mature and able to create the cycle once more.

STOATS AND WEASELS

Seemingly always in a hurry, either streaking across the road and woodland rides, or rippling sinuously along the hedgerows, these two fierce hunters rarely pause long enough to afford any prolonged observation. However, on one of those days when luck is on your side, you might disturb one or the other while feeding on a recent kill, which is most likely to be a rabbit. Showing little fear, the small assassin will hiss and spit its disapproval, then should you approach closer it will run off into the undergrowth to reappear at intervals, keeping up a constant barrage of chakkering abuse.

Both having red brown fur on the upper part of the body, and white on the underparts, there is little difference in their colouration. The main distinction between the two is that the stoat is considerably larger, about seventeen inches from tip to tip, is higher on its legs and has a longer tail which is black tipped. What the weasel lacks in size it makes up for in ferociousness and of the two is the more blood-thirsty. Only ten inches long, which includes its two inch tail, it will relentlessly

Stoat

pursue its intended prey and kill with a savage bite in the neck. Rats are a common prey and here the weasel's smallness is an advantage over the stoat for it is able to follow them down and through the labyrinths of their tunnels. Considering that a full grown rat can be over twice its size and equally as savage, it does say a lot for the weasel's courage.

In the main, general habits and life styles of stoat and weasel are virtually the same, so the following description can refer to both.

Mating takes place around February and the young, numbering on average four or five per litter, are born after a gestation period of forty days. These kits, measuring half an inch in length at birth, are typically blind and naked and do not leave the nest, which is normally situated in any ready-made dry hole or burrow, until they are fourteen days old. Development is rapid and they are soon assisting their parents on their hunting forays. When they reach maturity at two months of age they leave the family group, though it is not unusual for them to remain together for the whole year.

Generally – but certainly not exclusively – nocturnal, they spend their time either resting, or quartering their chosen area in an insatiable search for prey. Prey is sought by scent and hearing, for their sight tends to be somewhat myopic. Once located, attack follows brief stalking and ends in a short swift rush, the death blow invariably being a single bite behind the ear or at the base of the skull. No creature, apart from the larger carnivores, are safe from these little killers. Rabbits seem to have an instinctive terror of stoats or weasels, and a confrontation will often result in their nervous system becoming so deranged that they collapse in a paralysed state. It has been proved that in many cases rabbits have died of shock without any physical attack being made upon them, which probably accounts for stories of stoats and weasels being able to *charm* their victims.

Their diet is entirely carnivorous and, apart from hunting on the ground, they climb trees to take birds and eggs from the nest. They will also not hesitate to take to water in search of voles or fish. During harsh winters family packs hunt together and there is recorded evidence of dogs and even men being severely bitten having crossed the path of one of these savage parties.

Normally wary of contact with humans, during the winter they tend to draw closer to man, haunting farm buildings, systematically killing the occupants of lofts, byres, haystacks and potato caves; in fact, doing man a great service by keeping down rodent pests. This service is not often appreciated, for the corpses of countless stoats and weasels may be found ranging alongside the remains of foxes, hedgehogs, crows and others on the gamekeeper's *gibbet*.

While the weasel does have a metabolism to effect a change of fur colour during very cold weather, this is rarely used, as weasels favour more southern aspects of the country. Stoats however, which live in the mountainous districts of Scotland, where winter temperatures can reach arctic proportions, undergo this metamorphosis annually, turning them pure white, save for the black tip on the tail which never changes colour. As the stoat's method of killing is to stalk as close to its prey as possible before pouncing, it is obvious that unless it is camouflaged in white, hunting across snow would be virtually impossible due to its normal fur colour being so conspicuous. Though the change from brown to white seems to take place almost overnight, in fact the white has been growing under the normal coat, and is only suddenly revealed by a speedy moult brought about by a temperature drop. Incidentally, the fur in this white condition is known as *ermine* and as such is used for the trimming of robes worn by royalty, peers and judges.

Stoats and weasels belong to a classification group known as mustelidae, and included in this group are the marten and polecat, which is understandable. What is not so obvious is that the remaining two of this group are badger and otter. Yet, if you examine the six collectively, there are many facets which are similar.

MARTENS

At one time the pine marten was common all over Britain, but the same reason which drove the wild cat to the furthest extremity of the land, has now expelled the marten to such outposts as the Highlands, North Wales, the Lake District and parts of Ireland. In these areas it lives in wooded, mountainous districts, though contrary to its name, not necessarily in pine forests.

It is our most rare mammal, but as the persecution which decimated its numbers in the first place has been stopped for a number of years, it is now on the gradual increase. This is good news, for without doubt it is the most beautiful and graceful member of the mustelidae, if not of all our mammals.

However, pretty or not, like its relatives, the marten has a propensity towards wanton bloodlust, and because of this can cause great damage so far as poultry and game are concerned.

Not at all a difficult creature to identify, the marten is by far the largest of the *weasel types*, and may sometimes reach lengths in excess of thirty inches from nose to tail-tip. The body is slender, while the legs are short, but the hairy soled, sharp clawed feet are disproportionately large, enabling it to scale trees and other vertical surfaces with a breathtaking skill.

The fur is exceptionally beautiful, particularly in winter. Overall colouring is a deep rich brown, except for the throat and upper breast which has a *bib* of cream or yellow, though during autumn this is often pale orange. The tail is bushy and used in a similar manner to that of the squirrel, as a means of balance when leaping through the branches in pursuit of prey.

Food is largely sought above ground, and such is their fleetness and balancing skill that often fully grown birds are brought down, but generally it is the squirrel which falls victim to its rapacious ways.

Apart from squirrels, the marten favours mice, rats, rabbits, birds' eggs or chicks and, of course, domestic poultry, while it is not averse to whatever nuts or fruits are in season. Hunting usually starts at dusk and during a night foray a marten can, and does, cover as much ground as seven miles.

Except in bare, hilly country, where its nest would be in fissured rock, it generally chooses for its lair a hollow tree or the deserted nest of some high nesting species of bird such as carrion crow, sparrow hawk or magpie. The latter's nest is usually the favourite on account of the domed roof and narrow entrance. Having killed the tenants, a squirrel's drey is also favoured for similar reasons.

Mating takes place in July or August and the average litter of four white-coated kittens are born in the following April. At two months of age they are ready to leave the nest. At first they are seemingly afraid of heights, which rather points towards the arboreal habits of the martens being acquired rather than traditional.

At the base of the tail there is a scent gland which is used for marking out territorial boundaries. The resultant odour is by no means offensive and for this reason an alternative name of sweetmart may often be encountered.

POLECATS

In contrast the polecat has an alternative name of foumart, that is, foul marten, for its skin is made commercially useless by the evil odour which attaches to it, even after the pelt has been cured.

In many ways the polecat is similar to the marten. It is equally rare, but its demise was brought about not like the marten, for the quality of its fur, but because it was such a pest in killing for the sake of killing. Today polecats are mainly to be found in Wales.

In general physical shape it resembles the marten, though it is a bit smaller, measuring only twenty-two inches from tip to tail. The long coarse fur is black-brown, but the softer underfur is yellowish-brown, giving an overall colour of pale, chocolate-brown. The legs and head are black, while the mask, or face, has white markings which often merge together over the eyes during the winter.

Its diet is the same as the marten's, though as it shows no aptitude for climbing trees, only those squirrels and birds which may be caught on the ground figure on its menu. On the other hand, it will take to water without hesitation, so fish, and particularly eels, make up a high proportion of its food. A curious habit, and one not shared by its relatives, is the building up of larders of many of its victims. Mice, frogs and other small creatures figure prominently in these hoards. I have heard stories that frogs are bitten at the base of the skull by polecats in such a way as to cause paralysis rather than death, thus keeping a store of fresh living food, rather similar to the way in which moles keep worms. However, until it is proven beyond doubt, I shall keep an open mind about this.

A polecat will exterminate all the pheasants in a covert by killing the adult birds and devouring the eggs, and by the same token can empty a rabbit warren in a couple of nights. So one can understand why they have suffered continuous persecution.

Though quite capable of digging a home, the polecat rarely does, preferring instead to occupy a rabbit burrow or crevice in the rocks. Nomadic by nature it will not stay permanently in any one place and may change its home with the seasons, often retiring to a woodpile or disused building during the rigours of winter.

Polecat

In March the polecats pair and the female prepares a spherical nest with a single small entrance, which she lines with soft hair. The kits are born some six weeks later and, like the martens, are clad in soft white fur. Normal litter size is five or six. After bearing her young the *jill*, or female, entirely sheds and renews her coat; the male, or *hob*, does likewise, though more leisurely, later in the year. This shedding of fur results in a shorter, darker coloured – summer – coat.

At the risk of being pessimistic, I will say that you will be very fortunate indeed to catch anything more than a glimpse of either the marten or the polecat. Yet if you wish to study basic habits then you need do no more than watch or keep the domesticated ferret.

FERRETS

The dentition, or tooth structure, of a ferret, its habits and colour, are all so similar to the wild polecat that there is little doubt of their relationship. To further this point, ferrets and the true (wild) polecats will breed together and the resultant cross is fertile. If they were not closely related the offspring would be infertile as in the case of the mule, the cross between a donkey and a female horse.

Though domesticated for at least a thousand years, ferrets are far from tame, far from affectionate and seemingly always awaiting the opportunity to slip back into the wilds. This is why I am presenting this little animal in a book basically about creatures of the woods and fields, for there is a very good chance that you may happen across one. Escapees which have bred possibly run into many, many thousands.

There are two varieties of ferret – the polecat and the white – the latter being an albino, as shown by its pink eyes. In general appearance the two are similar – lithe, muscular, long-bodied and with sharp intelligent features, conforming, in fact, to the accepted mustelidae shape.

The polecat variety is usually larger, somewhat wilder, more agile and hardier than the white; therefore it is preferred for ratting, where savageness and agility are of particular value. However, its colouring which can vary from almost black, through skewbald to grey-white, can often be against it. Emerging from a burrow covered with sand, many a ferret has been chopped because an over excited terrier has mistaken it for a rabbit. So the white, though slower and occasionally less keen, has the advantage, at least, of being seen which is a great help for itself, terrier and man while working in dim woods or twilight.

The basic usage of the ferret is simple. First, all holes in a warren are covered with a large-meshed purse net, which is securely pegged to the ground. Then the ferret, first muzzled to prevent it killing and eating the rabbits, is introduced into any one of the holes. In their efforts to escape from the ferret's relentless progress, rabbits run out and are trapped in the nets.

Behaviour of the ferret once inside the burrow can vary with the individual. Some, particularly of the polecat type, are always in a hurry and seemingly incapable of wearying. Others are equally cautious, pondering each move at every given opportunity – I myself have owned one such beast, and can safely say that nothing is more irritating to the nerves than one of these dreamers. Having vanished for fifteen minutes, which to me appeared more like an hour, it would pop its head out of a hole, make idiotic grimaces peculiar to its tribe, then vanish for an even longer period.

Should a ferret meet a stranger of its own kind, or a stoat on the same business, they pass each other with an air of armed neutrality. Very seldom will they fight unless cornered together.

Whilst spreading fear wherever they tread, all the aforementioned hunters may often feel this emotion even more keenly themselves, because their attackers have the unfair advantage of wings. Generally it is the smaller carnivores that suffer depredation from birds of prey, but even the larger species can fall to talon and curved beak.

In a book of this kind I could not do justice to the appearances and habits of all our predatory birds. Therefore I will draw your attention to that group which has all the attributes of the tribe, whilst being a good deal easier for the amateur to observe.

OWLS

Owls are known to everyone – even to those who have never heard or seen them – on account of their characteristic note, though in truth the popularly known *hoot* belongs only to the tawny owl.

None of the five species of owl which breed in Britain are rare; three are common and widely distributed throughout the country. There is, in fact, a sixth owl which breeds here – the snowy owl – but so far this has only reared young on the island of Fetlar in the Shetlands and it can hardly count as a real part of our regular fauna.

While each species is distinctive in its own right, they all have certain attributes in common. Having forward facing eyes enables them to judge distances with unbelievable precision, for their vision becomes almost binocular. You might think that for a hunter, eyes which only look forward would be a grave disadvantage, but nature has not ignored this fact and owls have the incredible ability of being able to turn their heads in a complete arc, and so look directly behind them. Also they can see clearly in what to us would appear total darkness, for the retina of the eye is extremely sensitive to light. Coupled with this is the fact that they are completely silent in flight, because their wing tips are soft and so break up the air flow, the normal cause of wing noise. So you can see that their very make-up is directed towards them being superb, stealthy nocturnal hunters. Let us take a look at each species as an individual.

THE BARN OWL

Few birds are so strangely individual in appearance as the barn owl. The flat face – or facial disc, as it is known – is particularly well developed in this species. Yellow-brown around the edges it is almost perfectly heart-shaped, the heart being bordered and divided down the middle by a row of greyish spots. The rest of the disc is white, the feathers appearing to radiate in two groups from the long slanting eyes. The beak, strong and sharply hooked, is hidden within the centre by fine white feathers.

The underparts are white, spotted with dark grey. The upper parts are actually pale orange-brown, but each feather is so marked with grey that one gets the impression that grey is the general colour. The legs are a beautiful feature, and one shared by all the species, for as far down as the claws they are clad in downy grey-white feathers, making the owl appear to be wearing furry trousers. The barn owl is not particularly large and, indeed, you might be surprised just how slight it really is if you were to handle one. For while at rest, its puffed up feathers give an impression of size, and when in flight, its twenty-eight inch wing span, again, makes you think it is bigger than it is.

A very good friend to the farmer, it feeds chiefly on mice, voles, rats, starlings and sparrows. Beetles and other insects are also eaten in large quantities, many of them being caught in the air. All small prey are eaten whole, the bird half swallowing the creatures and digesting them slowly, bit by bit. So the sight of a barn owl with a tail or wing hanging from its mouth is not an uncommon one. Indigestible parts, such as fur and bones, are regurgitated in a compact mass known as a pellet. These pellets are to be found wherever any owl generally roosts and are certainly worth a close study. By gently teasing them apart and separating each item, you will be able to catalogue each creature which the owl ate within the last few hours. This observation, carried out regularly over a year, will give you a record of an owl's seasonal diet.

Dry pellets also form the sole lining of the nest, though in contradiction I must say that the barn owl makes no real nest as such, but instead lays its eggs, numbering from four to eight, on the surface of a roof joist, or in the base of a hollow tree. Apart from these situations, church towers, ruins, and cliff faces are used as accommodation.

The eggs are laid at intervals of three days, so should you be able to examine a nest you would find owlets of all ages. The young are covered with white down and are decidedly comical looking. Yet put your hand close and they will throw themselves on their backs ready to defend themselves fiercely with beak and talons.

THE TAWNY OWL

Next to the barn owl, the tawny owl is our best known, and though not as widespread as the former, certainly more common. Brown is the chief colour of this bird's plumage. The warm red-brown of the back is streaked and speckled with darker shades, and the secondary feathers have pale tips, which appear as bars across the wings. The underparts are pale, with longitudinal brown markings, the face is grey-brown and shaped like an inverted heart, though this disc is not as striking as that of the barn owl.

Essentially a woodland bird, it is seldom seen in open country. Moreover, it is less fond of hunting in twilight than the barn owl, which

Tawny Owl

can often be seen flitting silently, white and ghostlike, along the hedgerows as dusk is falling. Incidentally, this period between day and night is often referred to by countrymen as *owl-light*.

On a number of occasions my attention has been drawn to a tawny owl, which otherwise would have gone unobserved, by the fact that a number of small birds had discovered its hiding place and were diving at it, screeching and scolding their disapproval. Often these impudent passerines will harry the owl from tree to tree until they force it to flee the wood altogether. The owl, dignified as ever, makes no effort to retaliate, though I would imagine it mutters to itself *just wait until dark*.

The tawny owl is the true hooting owl, though the traditional *too-whit-too-woo* must surely have been a figment of some early writer's imagination, for no owl makes a sound such as this. The proper call is this – two preliminary *oo-oo*s followed by a long drawn out repetition of the same phrase. This is a beautifully musical sound, despite its eerie quality. The call is delivered by both sexes, whether on the wing or while the bird is stationary on roof top or branch. Another sound is the gutteral *ki-wik, ki-wik,* uttered by the owls when calling to each other on their hunting forays.

The cry of the barn owl is aptly described in its alternative name of screech owl. This extraordinary sound begins as a hiss and continues as a rising scream – nasal rather than throaty. But if the idea behind this heart stopping sound is to startle small mammals into movement, then I am sure the reverse effect is obtained, and they *freeze* into complete stillness. But, perhaps the owl has spotted its victim before screaming – so it would have the effect of holding the prey long enough for a death dealing swoop.

Food and nesting habits of the brown, wood or tawny owl – all descriptive names – are similar to the barn owl.

THE LONG EARED AND SHORT EARED OWLS

These terms are a misnomer, for the ears referred to are not ears at all, but are feather tufts – playing no part in hearing whatsoever. Their main use is decorative rather than functional, for they are used in courtship displays. When not in use they may be laid flat along the head. True ears are situated at the side of the head, and unlike our own ears for instance, are not in line. This lop-sidedness creates a time-lag between the arrival at each ear of the same sound wave, so helping the bird to accurately pinpoint the sound source. All owls have this feature.

Both owls are similar in size and colour, being roughly fifteen inches in length with buff plumage streaked with brown. Yet here similarity ends, for their life-styles are totally different.

The short eared owl hunts by day and favours such places as grassy, upland moors and lowland marshes. Its counterpart, like the tawny owl, only hunts during the hours of darkness and prefers the seclusion of coniferous woods; during the day it sits upright against the trunk of a tree, its colouring being such, that you might stare right at it and see nothing. Both are to be found more prominently in the northern half of Britain, though occasionally when the vole population in southern parts reaches high proportions, great numbers of short eared owls will be attracted to the south. More than any other species they have their range and numbers determined by food availability.

The short eared nests on the ground, laying its four to eight white eggs, in a simple depression, during April. The long eared takes over the nests of crows but egg colour and breeding times are similar to the former.

THE LITTLE OWL

Being only nine inches long, this owl is easily recognised. Also, being less nocturnal than most of its allies, it may frequently be observed perched on telegraph or fence posts during the daytime, even in bright sunshine. Introduced to Kent in the 19th century, it must have found conditions equal to, or better than, its natural continental home, for in no time at all it spread and colonized areas in England, Wales, and southern Scotland.

By preference it frequents more or less open country, breeding in holes in hedgerows, trees, pollarded willows, buildings or cliffs. Almost all its food is captured on the ground and consists principally of large beetles, insects, earthworms and small rodents – this you could check by searching for the aforementioned pellets.

Its cry is a monotonous, far-reaching *cu-cu-cu*, which at times could be called a mewing sound.

All owls are protected by law, for while it is accepted that they kill occasional game, their depredations of rodent pests far outweigh any harm they may cause. At one time it was common to see their lifeless bodies decorating gamekeepers' gibbets, but now this is a very rare sight.

A word of warning to those of you who might wish to study owls at close proximity to the nest, though this warning should normally only apply to the tawny. Either protect your face – particularly your eyes – or keep well away. For the tawny never hesitates to swoop and attack human intruders, and as this is done soundlessly you will have no warning. Well intentioned and experienced naturalists such as David Stephens and Eric Hoskins have both been severely taloned, the latter unfortunately losing an eye while photographing at a nest.

BIRD LIFE IN GENERAL

It is a mistake to suppose that our bird population shrinks with the departure of summer residents. Strangely enough while we certainly have less species, the actual number of birds is considerably more. The reason is this; nesting sites and food supplies for nestlings are limited in such a small island as Britain, therefore this controls the number of birds that nest here. But as these considerations do not apply in winter, we are able to subsist many more.

Because we have a plentiful supply of water, it is noticeable that the great majority of visitors and passage migrants are water-birds. However, no matter which habitat each species prefers, all are constantly on the move, following the food supply.

So in November the mixed finch flocks are to be seen in the beech woods, avidly searching for mast. Later, when frost has made the fields an unprofitable hunting ground, finches, sparrows, buntings and tits, with a robin or two on the outskirts of the group, visit stackyards in search of grain amongst trodden chaff and mud.

The tree-creeper and nuthatch work tree trunks, systematically searching the fissured bark for insects. So now, among the leafless trees is the time to spot them. Sometimes you might see them flying with the finches, but normally they are solitary. Not all of our birds wish to

A pack of **Knots** *flocking.*

flock together in winter – at least not when feeding. The tiny wren, meadow pipit, pied wagtail and the blackbird, rarely feed in company though they are never very far from their own kind.

As with most aspects of winter life, birds, too, are more easily observed, not least of all in your own garden, where a selection of food-stuff, i.e. nuts, fatty rinds, fruit and crumbs, will bring a host of rewarding sights. By the way, in really cold weather, don't forget to put out some water – replacing it when it freezes, for it is not usually the cold which kills thousands of birds every year, but lack of food.

While you may be cold, damp and mistbound when watching birds at the water's edge, it is invariably worthwhile – the conditions which make it difficult for you to see the birds make it equally difficult for them to see you.

A lake that in spring may carry a dozen pair of mallard and a dozen pair of coot, may carry as many as two hundred of each species in winter. In addition, there may be large flocks of teal, tufted duck, pochard, widgeon and so on, and you may be fortunate enough to catch sight of a smew, which, whilst not rare, is not all that common. You will certainly see goldeneye ducks wherever you carry out your spotting, and on the shores of marsh, mere, or streamside there will be a sandpiper or two, snipe, redshank and other waders. Look out, too, for that sentinel of the water, the heron – motionless, apparently asleep, but with dagger beak ready for action.

Assuming your bird watching enthusiasm is not dampened by blustering gales and lashing rain, keep an eye and ear open for our largest song bird – the mistle thrush. This beautiful thrush, instead of seeking shelter or huddling dispiritedly on some rain sodden branch, perches on the highest point of a tree and tries to out-whistle the wind, hour after hour, living up to its alternative name of storm-cock. So even in the bleakest hour of mid-winter, there is always a bright spot.

I am occasionally asked whether birds shelter in their nests during cold or wet weather. The answer is no, for while they naturally seek shelter, to them the nest is simply a nursery for rearing young and they do not return once this is over. Wrens sometimes crowd into an old nest – not necessarily their own, as they have been found in disused swallows' nests – but it is more usual for birds to roost in woods, wall-clinging ivy or buildings.

Ptarmigan

INDEX

Adder - 63, 159
Alder - 1
Algae - 152-153
Anemone - 32
Animal Play - 84-85
Ants - 88
Arrowhead - 48
Artichoke Gall -99
Arum - 35
Ash - 144
Autumn Bird Life - 125
Badger - 6, 7, 42, 74-79, 84, 140, 159
Baiting - 77
Balsam - 94
Bark Beetle - 68
Barn Owl - 172-173
Barren Strawberry - 32
Bats - 37-40, 140, 157
Bedeguar Gall - 99
Beech - 144, 154
Beech Tuft - 154
Belladonna - 96
Berries (Edible) - 91-92
Bindweed - 48
Bistort - 48
Bittern - 27
Blackbird - 1
Black Bulgar - 154
Bladderwort - 36-37
Bluebell - 48
Bog Moss - 151
Boletus Fungus - 34
Brambling - 127
Brimstone - 2, 157
Broom - 94
Buddleia - 85
Buds - 143
Bullrush - 50
Buntings - 71, 177
Burdock - 95
Buttercup - 48, 143
Butterflies - 47
Butterfly Bush (see Budleia)
Butterwort - 36
Campion - 143
Carrion Crow - 131-132
Catkins - 1, 2, 99
Catsear - 48
Celandine (Lesser) - 31
Celandine (Greater) - 32
Centipede - 64
Chakid - 100
Chanterelle - 154
Charcoal Burner - 151
Cherry Gall - 99
Chickweed - 2
Chough - 137
Cinquefoil - 48
Cleavers - 95
Clematis - 95
Clover - 143
Coltsfoot - 32
Coot - 24
Coypu - 123-125
Cricket - 87-88
Crocus - 143
Crow Family - 129
Cub Hunting - 108
Cuckoo - 10-12, 125
Cuckoo Pint - 34-35
Cuckoo Spit - 13
Currant Gall - 99
Daisy - 2
Damselfly - 52
Dandelion - 2, 95
Deadly Nightshade - 96
Death Cap - 154
Deer: Red, Roe, Muntjac, Chinese Water Deer, Sika, Fallow, Reindeer - 101-105
Devil's Bit Scabious - 143
Devil's Coach Horse - 64
Dipper - 1, 30
Dog Rose - 48
Dormouse - 6-9, 140, 157
Dragon Fly - 51
Dutch Elm Disease - 67
Edible Frog - 16
Eels - 113-114
Elder - 154
Elf Cup Fungus - 33
Elm Bark Beetle - 67
Fairy Ring - 155
Fat Hen - 48

Feather Moss - 150
Ferns - 52-53
Ferret - 170-171
Fieldfare - 127
Finches - 74, 177
Fire Weed (see Willow Herb)
Flies - 157
Fly Agaric - 154
Fox - 6, 42, 76, 84, 161-164
Foxgloves - 48
Frog - 14-16, 159
Froghopper - 13-14
Fungi - 33-34, 153-156
Galls - 98-100
Glow Worms - 88
Gnats - 19-20
Goldilocks - 150
Goosegrass (see Cleavers)
Gorse - 2,94
Grasshopper - 87-88
Grass Snake - 61, 159
Grasses - 53-55
Great Diving Beetle - 23
Great Grey Shrike - 127
Great Silver Beetle - 22
Green Woodpecker - 69
Groundsel - 2, 143
Hare - 81-84
Hawk Moth - 45-46
Hedgehog - 42, 137-140, 157
Hedge Sparrow - 1
Heliotrope - 32
Herb Robert - 92
Heron - 27-29
Holly - 145-146
Honeysuckle - 44-45
Hooded Crow - 131-132
Horse Chestnut - 144
Hounds - 110
House Martin - 72-73
House Sparrow - 74
Ivy - 145-146
Jackdaw - 134-135
Jay - 128, 135
Jews Ear Fungus - 154
Kingfisher - 6, 26-27
Lapwing - 74
Leaves - 96
Leveret (see Hare)
Lichens - 149-150
Little Owl - 176-177
Lizards - 59-61
Long Eared Owl - 175-176
Longhorn Beetle - 67
Long Water Scorpion - 23
Lords and Ladies - 35
Magpie - 6, 136
Marshfrog - 16
Marble Gall - 99
Marigold - 143
Marten - 167-168
Mayweed - 48
Millipede - 64
Mink - 122
Mistletoe - 148-149
Mole - 41
Montbretia - 48
Moorhen - 24-25
Morel Fungus - 34
Mosses - 150-151
Moths - 47
Musk Beetle - 67
Myxomatosis - 80
Natterjack Toad - 17
Nests - 2
Newts - 18, 159
Nightjar - 5
Nuthatch - 5, 177
Oak Apple - 99
Old Man's Beard (see Clematis)
Otter - 6, 85, 117-119
Owl: Barn, Tawny, Long Eared, Short Eared, Little Owl - 29, 171-177
Oyster Fungus - 154
Pansy - 143
Parson in the Pulpit - 35
Peacock Butterfly - 157
Peat - 151
Phalarope - 5
Pheasant - 13, 105-108
Pied Wagtail - 178
Pigeon - 74
Pike - 111-113
Pill Millipede - 64
Pimpernel - 95
Pipit - 178
Plankton - 152

Polecat - 168-170
Pond Skater - 22
Poppy - 48, 95
Rabbit - 6, 79-80, 159
Ramson - 48
Raven - 1, 130-131
Red Admiral - 85
Red-Backed Shrike - 127
Redpoll - 127
Redwing - 127
Reedmace (see Bullrush)
Reptiles - 58
Robin - 1, 71, 177
Robin's Pin Cushion - 99
Rook - 1, 28, 132-134
Rose Pea Gall - 100
Roundworm - 155
Saffron Milk Cup - 154
Salmon - 114-115
Sand Martin - 72-73
Sedge Warbler - 71
Seeds - 92-96
Sexton Beetle - 65-66
Sheep's Bit - 48
Shepherd's Purse - 143
Shrew (common) - 56-57
Shrew (pygmy) - 57
Siskin - 127
Skylark - 1, 73
Slow Worm - 61
Small White Butterfly - 2
Smooth Snake - 61
Snakes - 61
Snowdrop - 31, 143
Spangle Gall - 99
Sparrow - 5, 177
Sphagna Moss - 151
Squirrel - 6-7, 159
Spoon Bill - 27
Stag Beetle - 66
Starling - 5, 74
Sticky Willy (see Cleavers)
Stoat - 164-167
Stone Dweller - 64
Sugaring - 47
Sulphur Tuft Fungus - 33
Sundew - 35-36
Swallow - 72-73
Swift - 72-73, 125
Teazel - 51
Thread Moss - 33
Thrush - 1
Tinder - 154
Timberman Beetle - 67
Tits - 177
Toad - 15-17, 159
Toadflax - 48
Tortoiseshell - 2, 85, 157
Tree Creeper - 177
Trefoil - 48
Violets - 32
Viper (see Adder)
Wake Robin - 34-35
Wasp - 85
Wasp Beetle - 67
Water Boatman - 20-21
Water Measurer - 22
Water Scorpion - 23
Water Skater - 22
Water Vole - 120-122
Weasel - 164-167
Whirligig Beetle - 22
Whitlow Grass - 32
Wild Garlic - 48
Willow Herb - 95
Winter Fungus - 154
Witches Broom (see Gall)
Witches Butter - 154
Woodbine - 44-45
Wood Louse - 64
Woodpeckers - 42, 68, 70
Woodruff - 32
Worm - 158
Wren - 1, 178
Wryneck - 70
Yarrow - 143
Yellowhammer - 71